DR   INE

Land   s Guide

JERRY   **Land Surveyor**

R
UBLISHING

n, North Carolina

This book is designed to help the public understand important legal concepts of land ownership and to suggest solutions to problems encountered by landowners. We have done our best to give you accurate and useful information relevant to property ownership. Because laws change and vary from region to region, it is your responsibility to check all material you read here before relying on it. We assume no responsibility for errors, inaccuracies, omissions or any other inconsistency herein.

Editing by Susan Moncol

Illustrations by Ed Smith

Design considerations by Phil Bowie of Graphic Concepts, Inc.

Typesetting by Jack Owens of The Chapel Hill Press

TideRunner Publishing is committed to keeping its books up-to-date. Future editions of this book are planned that will provide even more help to landowners. You may call TideRunner Publishing to order the most current edition or printing. Special discounts for bulk purchases are also available for promotions and fund raising. For details contact:

TideRunner Publishing Co.
PO Box 770 (919)
New Bern, NC 28563 633-6649

Library of Congress Catalog Card Number: 93-79404

ISBN 0-9637828-0-0

dedication

Attempting to write a book and being short on writing skills could be a real handicap, were it not for good friends.

First and foremost, my sincere gratitude goes to Susan Moncol for assuming the albeit forced role of editor and critic. Special thanks to Phil Bowie for advice and help.

CONTENTS

Introduction

chapter 1
Influences From The Past   1

A LITTLE BIT OF HISTORY 1
    Early Land Ownership 1
    Statute of Fraud 3
    Roman Influences 3
TWO SYSTEMS FOR LOCATING LAND 4
    Metes and Bounds 4
    A Rectangular System For The Remaining Lands 6

chapter 2
Concepts of Ownership   9

THE TITLE SEARCH 10
THE SURVEY 10
WRITTEN METHODS OF TRANSFER 11
    The Deed 11
    Conclusion 11
UNWRITTEN METHODS OF TRANSFER 12
    Common Types of Unwritten Transfers 14
    Value of Unwritten Title 15
TRUE OWNERSHIP 15
    What is Evidence of Ownership ? 16
    Important Monuments 17
    Price of Missing Monuments 18
IMPORTANT LEGAL DEVICES 19
    The Quitclaim Deed 19
    The Property Line Agreement 20
    Save Money on Surveys 21
    A Question and Answer Overview 22

chapter 3
Real Estate Agent-Banker-Attorney-Surveyor 23

THE REAL ESTATE AGENT 23
    Ever-Changing Rules 24
    Referrals 25
THE BANKER 25
    Objectivity Can Be Important 26
    Saved From A Bad Deal ? 26
    Good Advice May Require Your Asking The Right Questions 27
THE ATTORNEY 28
THE SURVEYOR 30
    The Field Survey 30
    The Elements of Surveying 31
LEGAL AUTHORITY OF THE SURVEYOR 33
    Some Professionals Specialize 34

chapter 4
Contracts and Documents 35

INTENT TO PURCHASE 35
    A Close Look At An Important Contract 36
    Earnest Money 36
    Good Working Order ? 37
    Buyer's Options 38
    Seller's Options 38
    Is This Fair? 38
    Let's Make It Fair 39
    Food For Thought 40
HAZARDOUS AND TOXIC WASTE 41
    Don't Get Caught In A Dump 41
    Important References 43
THE TITLE SEARCH 44
TITLE INSURANCE 45
DEEDS AND THEIR PARTS 46
EASEMENTS 47
    Easements Cause Big Problems 49
    Exceptions Leave Something Out 49
THE LEGAL DESCRIPTION OF YOUR DEED 50
    Metes and Bounds Description 51
    The Beginning 52
    Another Beginning 53

chapter 5
Evaluating Deeds and Surveys 55

COMPARING GOOD WITH BAD 55
    The Good Survey 56
    The Bad Survey 58
    Basics Of The Survey 59
    Discrepancies Between The Deed and the Survey 60
    The Survey Provides No Legal Right 61
COMPARING THE LEGAL DESCRIPTIONS 62
THE SURVEY CHECKLIST 64
THE RECORDED DEED CHECKLIST 65
ONE FINAL WORD ABOUT YOUR DEED RECORDINGS 66

chapter 6
Your "MARKS" For All To See 67

MAKE IT PERMANENT 67
    Better Monuments 68
    Reference Stakes 68
CORNER WITNESS MARKERS 72
    Witness Monuments Are Versatile 73
CORNER WITNESS SYSTEM 74
    Triangulation 74
    Placing The Markers 75
    A Measuring Stick 76
    Materials 78
    Suggestions For Stake Substitutes 79
    Common Tools Needed 80
    Legal Considerations 80
    Finding Your Monuments 81
WITNESS MARKER RECORDING FORM (example) 82

Appendices   83

A — GLOSSARY OF SURVEYING AND ASSOCIATED TERMS............ 83
B — ALTA/ACSM LAND TITLE SURVEYS............................ 91
C — MEASUREMENTS AND VOLUMES 96

References   97

Index   99

Inserts   Rear of Book

Description "A" and Map "A"
Description "B" and Map "B"
Corner Witness Market Recording Form
Bonus Insert — "How To Save Money on Your Survey"

introduction

FOR THOSE WHO HAVE —
AND THOSE WHO WILL

It is the intent of this booklet to provide people who are purchasing land a guide to the proper steps and procedures of such a transaction. And for those who have already purchased property we will introduce and focus on methods to protect that investment. If you buy a VCR, television, car or almost any household item of relative value, you will receive an owner's manual advising how to use and care for the product. Even when you purchase an article of clothing a tag is included giving instructions for its proper care.

Is it not amazing, that in a world where an owner's manual is routinely supplied for nickel and dime items that the largest investment many of us ever make does not include even the first hint of instructions ? Are we to assume that everyone already knows all that needs to be known ? It seems unreasonable to make that assumption about something that is purchased only once or twice in a lifetime.

Hundreds of books have been written telling real estate people how to sell property, surveyors how to survey property, and lawyers how to research deeds and write legal descriptions of property. Some books have been written that tell people how to invest in real estate and/or a home. But, conspicuously missing from these publications is any serious treatment of how to protect that investment which encompasses the very foundation of the home - the property on which it is built. With the increasing value and scarcity of land today, it becomes important to be sure that you are doing and have done everything possible to protect that investment.

In order to accomplish this task we will focus on the role attorneys, surveyors, real estate agents, and bankers play in the initial purchase of property. I hope you will also gain insight into evaluating the work and selecting the right people for these jobs. But even more importantly, we will look at the work that remains to be done after these professionals have done their jobs. These will be things that you, yourself, can and should do to your property.

The legal right that we have in this country to own the land is envied by people of many countries. It is a valuable right and one that deserves safeguarding and constant attention. Our system of ownership works reasonably well, providing property owners a happy addition to their lives. But when the system does not work, problems of ownership can cause financial hardship and suffering. Many times a simple misunderstanding between adjoining owners can be cause for long-standing disputes between neighbors who may have once been friends.

Real estate agents, attorneys, and land surveyors are the chief providers of the services for the property owner and therefore must shoulder a great deal of the responsibility for these problems. Most professions provide their services in an ethical manner - but there are exceptions - those who do not care how they perform their jobs or are simply not capable of performing their work properly. After reading this booklet you should be better informed about how to secure the quality of service you deserve.

Books written for the professions are technical and usually filled with that profession's unique language and jargon. This booklet is intended for you the property owner. We will guide you through the process of the land purchase and show you ways to safeguard that purchase as simply and clearly as possible.

Please note that laws, customs, and practices can and will vary from state to state and county to county. Therefore, this booklet is meant as a guide rather than the authoritative source for your area.

chapter I

Influences From The Past

A LITTLE BIT OF HISTORY

The system to establish ownership of land in the United States evolved in large part from English and Roman common law. From the English we have the concept that written title to land is superior to the actual occupancy of the land. Roman law, on the other hand, provided that occupation gives superior control over the land. The merging of these and other historical concepts is similar no matter what part of the United States you live in. But leaving the roots of this system is very much like climbing a tree. The further up and out you go the shakier the branches become. Each state interprets the law regarding land ownership in subtle and occasionally not so subtle ways. It will be necessary to consult local sources for the specific statutes in your area.

Early Land Ownership

Some of the earliest accounts of land ownership and surveying can be traced back to Egypt and China roughly about 130 years B.C., but much of our system of land ownership originated in England. To understand how we got where we are we need but take a quick look at the English.

We begin in the year 1066, when William the Conqueror claimed all of the land in Great Britain as his own. William then gave half of this property to the lords and nobles who had fought with him. The estates of these lords were called "feudal estates" and naturally enough the lord became the feudal landlord. These landlords oversaw vast estates where tenants worked the land.

That land which was not owned or enclosed by the feudal landlords was called "Commons." Peasants were permitted to live and satisfy their basic needs on the Common lands. Unfortunately, much of these Commons were later taken over by the land-hungry lords until there was not enough land left for the peasants to subsist on. Additionally, William ordered a list to be compiled of every farm, owner, and tenant. This list was later to be known as the Doomsday Book, and became the first written basis for taxation.

With the "Statute of Frauds" passed by the English Parliament in 1677 it became necessary to show evidence of land ownership by a written contract. Today we call that contract a deed.

Statute of Fraud

Up until the sixteenth century it was nearly impossible for anyone not of noble birth to acquire title to property. Slowly this changed, and in 1677 an act of Parliament was passed that required contracts for land conveyances to be in writing and signed by the grantor. This act called the *"Statute of Frauds"* is at the very heart of our system of land conveyances today. These signed, written contracts are what we now call deeds.

Roman Influences

Although the English system gave us the precedent of showing written evidence to prove ownership of land, solving disputes over ownership was very difficult. To solve these problems we borrowed and incorporated from the Romans the concept of showing ownership through occupation. Today this concept can be related directly to adverse possession, which is discussed in the section under Unwritten Title.

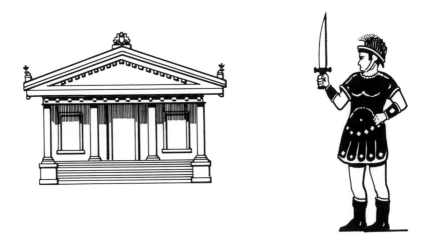

The Romans gained and occupied their land and property by force. This is the basis for adverse possession.

In early times ownership of land was reserved for a favored few. Today, ownership of land is enjoyed by many people. This right to own land is protected by more legislation than any other single right. As precious as this right of ownership is to Americans, and with property values continually escalating, delineation must be exacting, for there is no value in owning something which cannot be found or located.

TWO SYSTEMS FOR LOCATING LAND

If a recorded deed is a means of showing a contract between parties for the transfer of real property (land for our purposes) then there must certainly be a method to show what this real property is and where it is located. In this country we have two systems for referencing and locating land. The first and oldest system employed is called a "metes and bounds" system. The second is called a rectangular coordinate system.

Metes and Bounds

The metes and bounds system of describing land was the system used in Europe at the time America was first being colonized. It was and still is the primary system used in the first original 13 colonial states. A metes and bounds description is a description of real property which is not described by reference to a lot or block shown on a map, but is defined by starting at a known point and describing, in sequence, the lines forming the boundaries of the property. *Mete* means to measure, and *bounds* refers to the extents or limits of the property. Most often the extents or limits of the property are the properties of the adjoining owners.

A metes and bounds description can be very definitive as in this call (description of a property line); ...*thence a line N 35-48-35 E 325.28 ft., to an iron pipe corner, bounded by Sam R. Jones on the west and Bill Turnapple on the north.* Unfortunately, a metes and bounds description can also be very loosely defined; ... *thence in a direction up the holler with Jones line a distance of (3) three crow calls to a point near the head of Possum creek.*

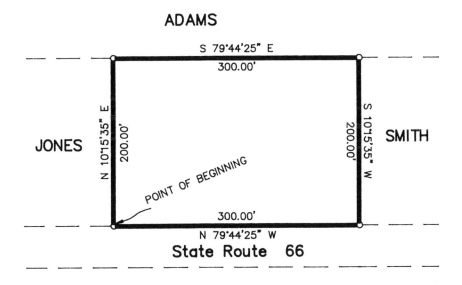

The "metes" of this property are the calls of bearing and distance on the property lines. The property itself is "bounded" by the properties of Jones, Adams, Smith, and State Route 66.

That last description with the three crow calls may be hard to follow but it may be a good description compared to the one that states: ... *being the property bounded by Jones on the west, Turnapple on the north, Smith on the east and Hooting Holler Ridge Road on the south.* This is an example of a bounds description. Amazingly, there are many properties today with just this type of description.

There were many problems in early America with land sales and the metes and bounds system. Many of the early settlers were given warrants (a form of deed) for a given quantity of land. The settler in those days simply went out, found a vacant piece of property he liked, and had it surveyed. In many of these instances the surveys would unknowingly overlap other surveys and claims. In the state of Georgia, 29 million acres of land were granted. The problem with this was that Georgia only contains nine million acres of actual land. The officials did a little better in North Carolina and granted only about twice as much land as existed in the whole state.

The shaded states on this map represent those states that were not a part of the early sectionalized land surveys. Except for Texas these were the original 13 colony states. The unshaded states were all a part of the public domain and subject to the sectionalized land surveys in one form or another.

A Rectangular System For The Remaining Lands

To combat these early problems, The Continental Congress developed a pre-survey system for the public domain. The public domain at that time consisted of most of the land west of the Mississippi River and comprised about three-quarters of the area of real property in the nation. In 1785, Thomas Jefferson was put in charge of a committee empowered to establish a land office for the United States. From this first land office Thomas Jefferson is given much credit for introducing the U. S. Rectangular system.

The early surveys of the west are often referred to as the "sectionalized land surveys." The idea for this system in its simplest sense was to establish a grid over and upon the land before it was sold or developed. The corners of this grid were to be established on the ground and were to act as the basis for future division of the larger squares into smaller parts. The largest division of the grid is called a township and is roughly six miles square containing 36 sections of land each roughly one mile square. As the divisions of land within the township become smaller and smaller, metes and bounds descriptions are used to describe the more irregular parcels.

6	5	4	3	2	1	1 MILE SQUARES
7	8	9	10	11	12	
18	17	16	15	14	13	section
19	20	21	22	23	24	
30	29	28	27	26	25	1/2 section
31	32	33	34	35	36	1/4 section

1 MILE ±

1 MILE ±

This figure illustrates a typical township and its 36 sections, which can be divided into smaller portions. Most sections are 1 mile square but due to errors encountered in applying this grid to a curved surface, the northern and western sections can be more or less than a mile.

The sectionalized land surveys in the 1800's were far from perfect. But considering the lack of technology and harshness of the environment at the time it is amazing that it was established as well as it was. Whether you live in a state which was divided by the sectionalized land survey or the metes and bounds surveys of the east, the federal government has established a nationwide control system throughout every state from coast to coast. Monuments with both horizontal and vertical information are becoming more and more numerous and exacting. Most states have taken this basic control and expanded it so that control monuments are available to almost any survey project today. The use of this control network has greatly enhanced the quality of surveys that are currently being performed.

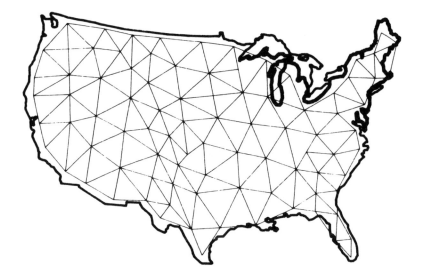

The Federal Government through the Coast and Geodetic Survey (part of the National Oceanic and Atmospheric Administration) established a control network across the continental U. S., Alaska and Hawaii. This control network consists of monuments placed on the ground with both horizontal and vertical data available. In addition most states further expand this network within the state to be more available to local surveyors and others. Although the grid is much more dense than represented here, it is a triangular network.

chapter 2

Concepts of Ownership

*You say you **own** this piece of land?*

Are you sure?

Can you prove it?

Do you need to prove it?

Once a prospective landowner decides to purchase a piece of property he hardly need lift a hand, other than his writing hand of course. From this point, the attorney, banker, real estate agent, and surveyor take over. In most instances, the new owner is led through the process - told what to sign - where to sign - and even occasionally why. Since most people only purchase property a few times in their life, it is important to have qualified people available to assist with these matters. The problem is they only help you in transferring title, with little or no instructions for the ongoing process of ownership, which begins after title is transferred. New owners are not even supplied with the first hint or set of instructions that could be useful in carrying out this process of ownership.

In this section we will take a quick look at how property is transferred so that there may be a better understanding of that process. The transfer process establishes the foundation for ownership. As with the foundation of a house it is important to insure that this foundation is constructed properly.

THE TITLE SEARCH

The reason for having a title search made is to find out if someone other than the seller has a legal claim to the property. More than once a piece of property has been sold to several people by someone having little or no apparent claim to the property. Rather than such obvious fraud sometimes these errors are simply created by an oversight in a previous deed. An unfortunate buyer could find that a forgotten heir of a previous owner has returned to claim their property. Only by having a title search done by a qualified person can we satisfy ourselves that the person we are dealing with is the rightful owner. Qualified persons are attorneys and title insurance examiners.

THE SURVEY

At this point you may have ordered a survey, because you need to locate the property to make sure that the property called for in the deed can be found on the ground. Sure, you've probably walked on a piece of property and been shown where the property lines are, but you really can't be certain until the surveyor has examined the seller's deed and found evidence on the ground to verify that it is, in fact, the same property.

WRITTEN METHODS OF TRANSFER

The Deed

Now that we've established that the seller appears to be lawful owner and that he is in fact selling us the property which he owns, we can proceed in having a deed made. What does the deed do for us? Well, it is a contract that says the seller (grantor) is conveying to you (grantee) his rights and interest to a certain property.

Conclusion

OK, you say I have a title search showing that the property I purchased was owned by the person I purchased the property from. I have a survey that shows the property I purchased was in fact the same property as called for in the deed. And I had a deed made showing that the seller transferred to me all his rights and interest to the property. Isn't that proof that I am now the owner of the property?

NO !! It is not proof !

It is merely bits and pieces of **evidence** which, used together, could prove that you own the property. The only place you can prove you own the property is in a court of law, and you do so by providing this evidence. Do not be misled into believing that just because you have a deed to property that it is proof that you own the property. A deed only declares that you have a legal claim to owning the property. It is but a piece of evidence.

This is an important concept to understand. What all the professions have done for you to this point is provide you with EVIDENCE that could be used to prove your ownership. If they have done their jobs well it is good evidence which will deter anyone else from laying claim to the same property. I hope that you will never need to prove in court that you are the rightful owner. But you must be prepared to do so, and this is the reason for having the title searched, the property surveyed, and the deed prepared and recorded. Obviously, the quality of these instruments might be important should you ever find yourself in court.

UNWRITTEN METHODS OF TRANSFER

Even though we go to all this time and trouble to own land, it must not be enough, because much land changes hands today through UNWRITTEN means, through *voluntary* and, more importantly, through *involuntary* methods. These methods can be acts of nature or acts of man that increase or diminish land areas. Though you've gone through the time and expense of having a written deed, not everyone does. In fact people can and do gain ownership of property without having to sign the first scrap of paper or pay the first dime of consideration.

Consider this excerpt from Curtis Brown's book, *Boundary Control and Legal Principles*. "The INITIAL right to land ownership in most states must be acquired by a written document; but after the original right is established by writings, land may be added to or subtracted from a person's holdings by unwritten means."

Additionally from this same source. " Unwritten Title Supersedes Written Title. Principle. Land lawfully gained by unwritten means extinguishes written title rights."

These are two important and powerful statements that should not be taken lightly. What these statements are effectively saying is this. Even though you may follow all the prescribed steps for acquiring written title to property, any and all of that property can be taken from you by methods that do not involve signing the first piece of paper. These unwritten methods can and often do represent an even stronger claim to ownership than can be provided by your written deed.

Let's examine why this is so. Everyone has heard the expression "Possession is nine-tenths of the law." Well this expression can be applied to property but we may word it just a little differently. Possession and occupation (maybe for a required time) is nine-tenths of the law. The law provides that we can become the lawful owners by meeting certain criteria. Only one or two elements are needed to satisfy these criteria; possession and/or time of possession.

The property owner of today must have written evidence of ownership (by deed) and should be prepared to show ownership through occupation. Occupation can be shown easily enough by delineating your property from others. This delineation should be physically visible on the ground by the use of corner monuments, fences, hedges , ditches, etc..

Common Types of Unwritten Transfers

Most unwritten property transfers can be traced back to two predominant methods. They are *"acquiescence and adverse possession."*

To *acquiescence* is to assign or give by consent. The key here is the word consent. Consent does not necessarily mean voluntary or vocal consent. An act of silence can be construed as an act of consent.

Adverse possession is in its simplest sense to "take or steal." Adverse possession can be traced back to the Roman Common Law, where a part of the spirit of the person possessing the land was transferred onto the land. Thus the person and the land became sort of part and parcel.

By not saying anything this couple may be giving away or acquiescing a portion of their property to their neighbor.

Simply knowing the definition of the law would be insufficient without knowing how the law is interpreted and applied, especially since interpretation will differ from region to region. It is important to be aware that unwritten methods of ownership do exist and to know that the written instrument, the - *deed* - has limitations.

Value of Unwritten Title

Gaining property by any of these methods can produce a claim of ownership that is superior to written title. But it does have drawbacks. Property owned by these methods does not have a marketable title in the eyes of the title insurance companies. If these companies will not insure title, then the property has a lesser value on the market. A marketable title can only be obtained by going to court to prove that you are the owner through unwritten means. If successful, you then have a court decision that does provide you with a marketable title. Obviously such a procedure could prove expensive, time consuming, and chancy.

TRUE OWNERSHIP

The deed itself provides evidence to the initial right to land ownership. Ownership is provided for in our legal system *foremost* by occupation and use of the land. This does not mean that you must build upon and work the land to its edges to prove ownership. But it does mean that you should delineate your property from others to substantiate your claim to ownership. And this delineation should be a constant and physical delineation. Probably no one in his right mind wants to find himself in a court of law for a property dispute, but there is always that possibility. The best way to avoid or reduce the odds of it happening to you is to be well prepared.

What is Evidence of Ownership?

As we may be called upon to show evidence of ownership some day, maybe we should take a look at what the evidence is and what to do with it. As stated above, the deed provides a legal basis for our claim and the survey map shows the evidence available to support that claim. Property corner monuments physically found and located on the property, and MATCHING what is called for in the deed description are the best form of evidence to prove your occupation, and therefor your ownership.

Remember, property lines are invisible. The monuments placed at the intersection of these invisible lines are the only physical evidence of their existence. There are other things which can be used to support or hypothesize the location of property lines, such as ditches and fences, but the corner monument represents the best evidence.

When corner monuments are not available, a person could easily use or build over the property line unknowingly. If his use or building is there long enough he could gain title to that property through acquiescence or adverse possession. Almost all states have a time requirement to gain property through adverse possession. That time can range from a low of five years in some states to 20 years required by others. But these time requirements can be misleading. A court could very well rule in favor of the trespasser if they felt he made an honest mistake and depriving him of the property would create a hardship. He would probably be required to compensate you for the property if he did not meet the requirements for adverse possession or acquiescence. That may not represent a very satisfactory solution if you wanted to keep the property. The courts take a much harsher view of a trespasser who crossed over a property line when that property line was reasonably apparent.

To avoid losing property through Adverse Possession or Acquiescence may require that you confront those that trespass across your property lines.

Important Monuments

If you are beginning to recognize the importance of those monuments placed at your property corners, congratulations. Understanding their importance should also prompt you to want to preserve their existence. If the property corners were known and visible to property owners at all times, there would probably be few land disputes today. To allow your property corners and monuments to become lost or in disrepair not only diminishes your claim to the property but exposes that property to unwritten methods of possession by others.

Price of Missing Monuments

In my years as a land surveyor I've noticed that a survey cost can range from a couple of hundred to several thousand dollars on seemingly identical properties. In nearly all these surveys one common problem determines the difference between the costs. Missing or lost corners. When your corner monuments are lost or destroyed, a surveyor must then rely on your neighbor and/or your neighbor's corner. Will they be correct? If not, there is a good chance your corners will not be placed in the same position in which they once stood. Surveyors like detectives must rely on evidence they find on the ground. If that evidence is faulty there is a good chance the results will be faulty too.

Do not be misled into believing that once monuments are placed they will always be there when you need them. They disappear for various reasons; some were never installed permanently enough in the first place, some were made of material that was not suitable for the conditions and permanence required, and others are lost to landscaping, logging, or regular yard maintenance. Still other monuments are not lost at all but are hidden as our memory of them becomes clouded with time and changing conditions.

IMPORTANT LEGAL DEVICES

Two of the best legal devices available to the property owner are the Property Line Agreement and the Quitclaim Deed. Adjoining property owners who wish to settle an unclear boundary, or change the boundary between them, can do so by using one of these legal devices. The Quitclaim Deed is the more commonly used device to establish a new boundary when the location of the old boundary line is known. But where the location of the property line is not known the Property Line Agreement may be one of the most valuable, overlooked, and underused legal tools available to the property owner. Attorneys will often use this device to legally bind and show the settlement results from a property dispute. The truly beautiful thing about the Property Line Agreement is that you can use it before a dispute ever arises.

An attorney should be used to help you draw up these deeds. If you use these instruments to transfer property, you may need to notify the lending or mortgage company before doing so. In the following pages we will take a closer look at the Quitclaim Deed and Property Line Agreement and when and how these instruments can be used.

The Quitclaim Deed

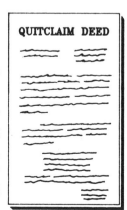

The Quitclaim Deed is probably one of the most commonly used forms for conveying title to properties. By simply deciding where you want your property line to be, adjoining property owners can make it so by signing Quitclaim Deeds. Each owner must sign the deed, transferring any and all rights they have to the property on the other side of the agreed boundary line. The deed must be recorded in the county land records office.

Additionally the line that they agree to must be physically evidenced on the ground. The physical evidence can be boundary markers, such as corner monuments placed at or along the line, or it can be a fence, ditch, or hedge along the line. You do not need a surveyor to locate the exact corner or intersection of the property line as you can define the line itself with the true intersection to be located at a later date. The Quitclaim Deed should be used only when you wish to change a <u>known</u> boundary line.

The Property Line Agreement

The Property Line Agreement can be used for many varied reasons and purposes. It is most often used to settle the location of a property line that is in question or doubt. Should two property owners decide that a property line belongs at a certain location, they can merely make that decision, sign a properly worded and notarized agreement, and the property line belongs at that location. This is possible in many states as long as no other parties are involved and certain legal recording requirements are met. Regardless of legal requirements of your area ALL agreements of this manner should be recorded, just as you would record a deed.

A property line is in dispute when the adjoining owners cannot find its location through reasonable inspection. Reasonable inspection does not require that you must hire a surveyor to try and locate the line. Many times a surveyor is called in to locate a property line that is old and very difficult to find. This can lead to a great deal of expense because of the time required. Property owners who can come to an agreement as to where they think the line should be can save themselves much money and time by signing a Property Line Agreement.

We must make a distinction between the Property Line Agreement as used in an unwritten method of transfer versus the property line agreement as a written method of transfer of property. In many states the property line agreement by unwritten methods is not a valid agreement if the boundary line can be ascertained from the deed or survey. To be used as an unwritten method the property line must be in dispute, uncertain, and unfixed. The property line agreement used in this fashion represents a real ticking time bomb to property owners. The solution is to write it down and record the agreement.

The written agreement must also conform to rules of a contract containing words of conveyance and consideration. All further reference to Property Line Agreements in this booklet will be in the form of agreements that are to be placed in writing and recorded with the proper land offices.

Together the Quitclaim Deed and the Property Line Agreement offer reasonable people an easy, inexpensive method of fixing a questionable property line or changing a known property line.

Save Money on Surveys

You may not want a surveyor to spend a lot of time and money trying to locate a property line that you and your neighbor can agree to. But you certainly should have a surveyor locate the new agreed line once it is established. Otherwise you may find yourself back where you started in a few years. With both the Quitclaim Deed and the Property Line Agreement, the line that is agreed to must be physically evidenced on the ground.

A Question and Answer Overview

QUESTION	ANSWER
How do I know that the person selling me the property actually owns all the rights and interest to the property?	Title Search
How can I protect myself from someone having other or even additional rights and interest to the property?	Title Insurance
How do I know that the description of the property in the deed will fit or that it even exists on the ground?	Property Survey
How do I show that the seller wishes to convey to me his rights and interest to the property?	Deed

After having done all these things the most important thing remaining is to show your ownership. Showing ownership need not be more than maintaining your property corner monuments. Establish a yearly schedule to visually inspect the monuments and their condition. In chapter 6 we will look at ways to repair and replace monuments when necessary.

chapter 3

REAL ESTATE AGENT - BANKER
ATTORNEY - SURVEYOR

As property owners and purchasers we use the services of many professionals. Real estate agents and bankers play an important role in the selection and financing of the property while attorneys and surveyors provide the services which lay the ground work for property ownership. In the case of attorneys and surveyors, the general public has a good idea what they do, but a rather limited concept of the actual importance and significance of their roles. On the other hand, the general public has a good idea of the real estate agent and banker's roles, but probably not so apparent are some of the more intangible services and knowledge these two professions can supply.

THE REAL ESTATE AGENT

Although a real estate agent may not be needed by everyone or for every transaction, a good agent can be very helpful. First and foremost, if the agent knows the market well, he or she can certainly save you much time and aggravation in trying to locate the right property. But that should not be their only service to you. They should be familiar with the many current and pending laws and regulations which could affect the property and ultimately your decisions.

Ever-Changing Rules

In coastal areas, many regulations have been written and continue to be written and revised concerning not only coastal wetlands but also what are called upland wetlands. The need for wetlands protection has created much debate and concern, and the continually changing regulations have also created much confusion. One thing, however, is certain: The impact of current and future regulations will have a devaluating effect on properties containing these wetlands.

As this booklet is being written, implementation of a "mandatory seller disclosure" law is being discussed. Although there may already be "disclosure laws" on the books of many states, this newly proposed law would extend the liabilities more directly to the seller than previous laws. Because of these and other regulations, selling and purchasing property today is not the simple matter that it was yesterday. While utilizing the services of a real estate agent may have been only an option in the past, the services of a good real estate agent today may be a wise and prudent decision in the face of the ever changing laws and regulations affecting our lives and property.

In addition to helping you locate the right property, your agent will also help you determine a reasonable price through their knowledge of the local market. After you've found the property and settled on a price, a lot of work remains before the final closing. Most successful agents work with the potential buyer closely until this time. Their experience can be invaluable in helping you coordinate what can be a maze of events and paperwork.

Referrals

Just as a good agent should know his market he should also be familiar with many of the professionals providing services you will need. These would include attorneys, surveyors, and bankers. Ask your agent to supply you with a list of capable professionals to contact. Do not be surprised that his list may include several persons of the same profession. This is considered good policy and avoids any risks of collusion or improprieties among the professions.

THE BANKER

The next step in your decision to purchase property is usually a trip to a bank. The right combination of lending institution and property can be key in obtaining a loan. Ask your Realtor for suggestions. Many publications have been written about how to find and finance property and except for this brief excerpt we will leave that subject to them. What we wish to pursue here are other avenues through which the banker can be of service.

In today's world, many banks are saddled with property loans gone sour. The current forecast for property values to increase with time is certainly more in question today than ever before. Because of this situation, expect the banker of today to be more cautious and wary than the banker of yesterday. Try not to view him as an adversary; his caution may be well-founded, and his rationale can provide you with an objective view which can be very beneficial.

Objectivity Can Be Important

An often overlooked and valuable service which the banker can provide is this objective view on a subject that may become overly emotional. Beyond this objectivity, a banker may possess little-known information about the particular area where the property is located. Perhaps there are factors that are suppressing the value in that area. For example, a selected type of housing unit may be performing poorly in response to market demands. The banker may have knowledge of undisclosed plans that may affect an area's future stability. Often a bank may have financed other properties in area in which you are interested. This can provide an excellent basis for evaluating the price you should expect to pay for the property.

Saved From A Bad Deal?

I cannot help recalling a time that I became interested in a condo unit that I found particularly appealing. The price of the unit was such that I felt it would make a superb investment for the future. With these thoughts in mind I visited a local banker. Fortunately, the banker was very frank and provided me with much valuable information.

The small community in which these units were situated was experiencing great difficulty with the expense of providing water and sewer services. Because of the condition of the present system they would be forced in the near future to upgrade the services and pass along a large rate increase to property owners. Not only could a rate increase be expected from the utility company, but it was also pointed out that the property owners' association had continually increased its fees and was likely to continue to do so. And if this wasn't enough, the banker related that sales of those and other condo units in the area had been slow and might continue to be so. A check on other units they had financed showed the price to be only slightly higher than what others had paid for their units. It also seemed likely that many future units would be devalued. I soon lost my interest in this wonderful investment I had planned to make and considered myself fortunate to have a relationship with a banker of such knowledge.

Good Advice May Require Your Asking The Right Questions

In other words, do not overlook this valuable source of objectivity and knowledge. Do not wait until the last moment to approach the banker for a loan. Discuss early on your intentions and seek out his or her advice and knowledge. Often a banker may possess knowledge he doesn't even realize you need or want. Many times it is up to you to ask the right questions to find the crucial answers. Do not hesitate even if the questions sound dumb. A relationship with a banker may not only provide you with money for a sound investment, but also save you the emotional and financial distress of making a poor investment.

Thus far in our discussions we have examined the potential interaction between the prospective landowner, the real estate agent, and the banker. The result has been to locate a desirable piece of property and to secure financing for the purchase. From this point we must look at preparing the information necessary to finish the process in what is commonly called the property CLOSING.

The closing encompasses preparing the information necessary to complete the legal documents required by law. For this final process the prospective owner will interact primarily with the attorney and the surveyor. What is needed to prepare the closing documents will be discussed in the following chapter.

THE ATTORNEY

From the time you begin to sign papers committing you to the purchase of your newfound property you are going to need the services of an attorney. The intent to purchase contract is usually the first contract to be signed and is probably one of the most important. It is usually signed before most people hire an attorney, but a good real estate attorney can be a real asset prior to the signing of this contract. As you will see in the next chapter it will often be to your advantage to modify the intent to purchase contract to better protect your interests. A good attorney will have sound advice and suggestions to help you with this.

Before the actual closing, many documents must be prepared by the attorney. The care and attention to detail in these documents are important because they establish the necessary evidence to create a strong foundation to support your claim of ownership. Among the attorney's many responsibilities are preparation of the title search, certificate of title, deed description, recorded deed, and deeds of trust as needed. He should also help arrange your insurance needs, financial contracts, survey needs, and a host of other miscellaneous documents.

Not only is the attorney directly responsible for preparing many of the documents listed above but he is also the orchestrator of the purchasing process. The attorney who does his job well will make all these things come together harmoniously.

If, however, things are not done in the proper sequence and in a timely manner, this process can be most frustrating. This will quickly become apparent when the date for closing goes by and you must rearrange new financing. Most lending institutions lock in an agreed interest rate for a limited time (usually 30 to 60 days) to allow for the closing. If you arranged the financing and locked in a good interest rate, it may be discouraging to find that interest rates have gone up and your purchase may now cost thousands more than anticipated.

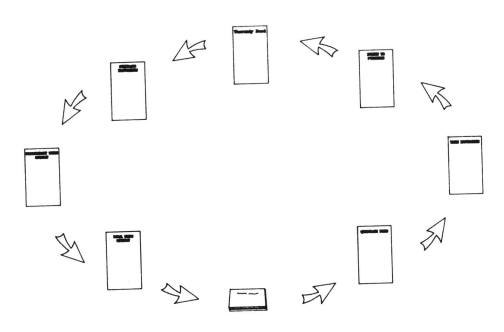

The attorney must bring together the completion of many documents and papers before the final closing date.

THE SURVEYOR

The surveyor has three primary duties to the property owner. These are to locate the property, investigate its condition, and report his findings accurately by means of a survey map.

To locate the property the surveyor must do research in the courthouse not only of the property to be surveyed but also on adjoining properties to make certain there are no overlaps, voids, or other problems that may affect your property. He must also be aware of Easements and Exceptions that may be necessary to locate on the ground. Much of this same research is done when the attorney or title search company does the title search. To avoid duplication make sure the title search is done far enough in advance to provide the surveyor a copy. It may not eliminate all the surveyor's research but it should eliminate a large portion, thereby reducing his time and expense to you. Only after thorough deed research is the surveyor fully prepared to do the actual field survey.

The Field Survey

When a survey crew comes to the property they normally try to locate as many monuments as they can find based upon the deed descriptions or map referenced in the deed. Monuments are those objects which are used to designate property corners. They can be artificial or natural monuments. Artificial objects could consist of; iron pipes, iron pins, re-bars, concrete cylinders or blocks, or a rock or stone placed for such purpose. Natural objects could include; trees, water courses, or natural rock outcrops existing but not placed by man. In addition to locating all existing monuments on the client's property, the crew will also locate many monuments on adjoining properties.

After corners and their monuments are located, all significant structures on the property should be locate 1. The surveyor should note and locate any unusual evidence that could suggest se or occupation other than what is thought to be the true property lines. Many things can suggest overlaps or use by others of property lines. Fences, roads, ditches, buildings that encroach and that are being used by others should be a red flag and suggest further examination. Problems of this nature should be noted and remedies should be sought from consultation with the surveyor and the attorney.

The Elements of Surveying

In times past a surveyor in the process of surveying a property would set up his transit over a property corner turn an angle and pull a tape or chain to measure the distance to the next corner. He would repeat this process at each corner until he had returned to the beginning. Unfortunately for him the actual property lines which he had to measure are usually the hardest and harshest places to traverse on the whole property. Judgements were made on the site then and there, and since calculations were laborious and lengthy, they were reduced to bare necessities. Errors in chaining were particularly common, and judgements were often based on limited evidence.

Today's surveyor may not set his transit directly over the property corner. Instead he can select sites that offer more convenience and allow the field work to progress much faster. Chaining and taping have now been replaced by electronic distance measuring which greatly speeds the gathering of information. The initial trip to a site is normally for information gathering only. Few if any decisions or judgements are made at this time. Instead the information is then returned to the office where with the aid of modern computers, calculations are reduced to a fraction of the time it used to take.

This method allows the surveyor to consider all the information as a whole, allowing him to make better judgements and decisions for corner replacement. A survey is never finished until missing monuments are replaced.

The technical aspects of surveying can be taught by our schools but the art of surveying must be learned by working with other surveyors. Unfortunately this profession has neglected the need for a structured apprenticeship program for the surveyor in training. As a result of the current inequality in training of surveyors, there is considerable difference in the quality of the products produced by individual surveyors. One of the major reasons for this is that there is no consensus among surveyors themselves on how the very basic nature of the survey should be conducted.

In one camp is the surveyor who believes he is doing his job by measuring what is on the ground and preparing a map of those measured bearings and distances, ignoring the deed description. In another camp is the surveyor that constantly shows only what is recorded by the deed and does not report the differences that often occur with what is actually on the ground. Even worse there is one brand of surveyor who decides to pick and chose between the deed line or the measured line, as to which he will show on his map.

The good surveyor will look at even a four sided lot and realize that their are a minimum of eight possible property lines. Four that were created by the deed and four that are created by the occupation of the property. If all things are as they should be all lines will merge into the four lines created by the deed. If however the lines of occupation differ from the deed he will show these as additional property lines along with the deed line. The area of the property between the deed line and the line of occupation should be noted and labeled "Property Occupied by Others" or with some other suitable wording.

By doing this the surveyor has alerted the current owner that there may be a problem that deserves his attention. For a new buyer it notifies that he may not be acquiring all of the property called for in the owner's deed. The surveyor has no way of knowing if the property in question has been transferred by written or even unwritten methods so his obligation is to alert others to the problem so that <u>they</u> can fix the problem if there is in fact one. Remember only the property owners and/or the legal system have this authority.

Many surveys are now being ordered by the attorney or real estate firm handling a property transfer. This may not be in the best interest of the buyer and for this reason I would suggest that someone buying property request the survey themselves. They may want to emphasize that they expect the survey to show any problems or differences that exist with the deed, adjoining deeds, lines of occupation, and the acreage of the area affected. There should not be any additional charge as this is what the survey is supposed to do. The surveyor should not represent either buyer or seller but should be completely unbiased in his report.

A smart landowner will address any problems that may affect the property well before a survey is done so that their are no problems to be disclosed by a survey that might threaten a future sale of the property. He does so by applying some of the methods described in chapter 6 for insuring that the property lines are marked and apparent. When property lines are marked and apparent it is then much easier to address any encroachments as they occur rather than years after the fact.

LEGAL AUTHORITY OF THE SURVEYOR

Although surveyors sometimes make judgments as to which corners are correct and which are not, they are not vested with any legal authority that dictates that their decisions must be honored or upheld. Their function is only that of reporting the evidence they find to support their conclusions as to the location of property lines. If a decision is required to establish a property line or resolve a dispute, that decision is reserved exclusively to the legal system. Property surveying is not an exact science as it relies greatly upon the experience and judgment of the surveyor. Because of this it is not uncommon for two different surveyors to come to two entirely different conclusions.

Exception to the above paragraph can be made in the case of property disputes by agreement of the property owners themselves. Should these owners agree by written consent, they could chose to have their property disagreement settled by an independent and mutually agreed upon surveyor. This would of course bind the owners to accept the decision and/or solution generated by the surveyor. If more people availed themselves of this method of settling their disputes, they could save themselves much time, money, and the frustration of using the court system. Many times after going through the courts to settle property disputes, the costs have far exceeded the actual value of the property that was in dispute.

Some Professionals Specialize

Keep in mind, not all attorneys or surveyors specialize in property transfers and surveys. Some attorneys may specialize in criminal law, some corporate, or perhaps contract law. Many survey and/or survey/engineering firms may be more geared toward construction surveys, rather than property surveys. Find the ones who do specialize in the area you're concerned with, as they will provide a better, more efficient, and often times less expensive service. The best way to find out who these people are is from referrals. Do not hesitate to ask.

chapter 4

CONTRACTS AND DOCUMENTS

The last chapter gave a brief introduction to the people that provide the services to property owners. This chapter examines these services and their products in detail. We begin where the new prospective owner would begin, and try to maintain the same order and sequence of the actual transaction phase.

INTENT TO PURCHASE

One of the most important things you are going to do when purchasing property is to sign a contract declaring your intentions to purchase. This is not something that you should rush into without first understanding what you are signing. If you are working with an agent they will probably explain and recommend changes to a contract to better suit the situation. An attorney would also be an excellent source of help and advice on this matter.

Most real estate agents use standard contract forms that are supplied to them through their associations. Do not assume that just because it is a standard form that it does not need revising. Precisely because it is a standard form it will almost always need revisions, deletions, and additions. Pay close attention to even the smallest words and details of the contract. Their meaning could be very important.

A Close Look At An Important Contract

The contract agents typically used is often called "Offer To Purchase and Contract." Although most of this booklet deals with land only, we will broaden our spectrum to look at this contract for someone would who is purchasing both land and house. We will not spend any time with the front of the document as it primarily addresses the essential elements required of a contract. It is the back side, with the small print, titled; "Standard Provisions," that deserves close inspection. Only those provisions which hold special interest will be examined. Some of the provisions will be discussed in detail; others we will only generalize about.

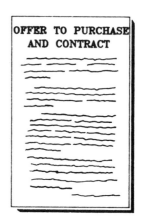

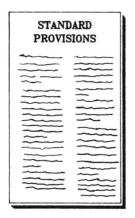

Earnest Money

Earnest Money is almost always the first provision in all real estate intent to purchase contracts. It states that you as the buyer will be required to provide earnest money as a show of good faith. This provision also establishes that if you the buyer breach this contract that you will forfeit that earnest money. It also establishes that should the seller breach the contract that the earnest money will be returned to the buyer. It is certainly not unreasonable to expect the buyer to put up a small amount of money to show his intentions and good faith. But let us reserve our analysis and conclusions about this provision until we've studied it and some of the other provisions.

We will skip some provisions and move directly to an important provision designed to protect the buyer and assign the responsibilities of the seller. Let's see how it does that.

8. INSPECTIONS: Unless otherwise stated herein: (i) the electrical, plumbing, heating and cooling systems and built-in appliances, if any, shall be in good working order at closing;...

(skipping a few lines)

... Buyer shall have the option to have the above listed systems, items and conditions inspected by a reputable inspector or contractor ...

(skipping a few lines)

Seller shall have the option of (a) completing them, (b) providing for their completion, or (c) refusing to complete them. If Seller elects not to complete or provide for the completion of the repairs, then Buyer shall have the option of (d) accepting the Property in its present condition, or (e) terminating this contract, in which case the earnest money shall be refunded. Closing shall constitute acceptance of each of the systems, items and conditions listed in (i), (ii), (iii), and (iv) above in its then existing condition unless provision is otherwise made in writing.

Good Working Order?

Let's take a close look at exactly what this Provision has done. First the seller is responsible for having the electrical, plumbing, heating and cooling systems and built-in appliances, if any, in good working order. What does good working order mean? Do these three little words mean the same thing to everyone? I don't think so; in fact I would venture to say that to some people it could mean that as long as things are working, no matter that they be held together with chewing gum and tape, they are in good working order. You may want to define what "good working order" means to you. Be aware that this provision gives permission for inspecting only those things listed above. What about the structural integrity of the building, or the land that goes with the building?

Buyer's Options

"Provision 8," gives you the buyer the option to have an inspection of the electrical, plumbing, heating and cooling systems and built-in appliances. This is an important option to exercise but it can represent an expense of several hundred dollars to the buyer. Most buyers are required by lending institutions to have this done and the buyer does usually pay. If an environmental inspection and/or survey needs to be done then it is possible to incur expenses in the thousands. As you will see under "Seller's Options," even if the seller is aware of any defects and doesn't disclose them to you before the inspection his only risk is your money.

Seller's Options

Now we come to the part of the seller's options concerning repairs to the faults that the inspection reveals. Article (a) and (b) states that the seller can complete or provide for the completion of the repairs. Article (c) of this provision provides that the seller will not be required to fix those things that the inspection revels. This is the ultimate loophole and provides the buyer with a new set of options. The buyer can now elect to accept the property in its present condition or terminate the contract and have the earnest money returned. But what about the expense the buyer has incurred? Inspections don't come free and although they may be a smart investment they are not cheap.

Is This Fair?

If the buyer feels he's getting a raw deal with "Provision 8," he'd better make an amendment to the contract that reimburses him for all expenses incurred should the seller be the one to breach this contract. The seller is protected by "Provision 1," of this contract with the buyer's forfeiture of earnest money should the buyer breach the contract. I do not think it too much to ask that the buyer is at least protected in some way for his expenses should the seller breach the contract.

Let's Make It Fair

OK, enough of this contract bashing. Let's see if we can't come up with some amendments to this contract that make it fairer to both buyer and seller. The following amendments represent a few of the standard changes that I, personally, would consider making to this contract. Pay particular attention to additions concerning toxic waste

Amendment to PROVISION 1. EARNEST MONEY: The first sentence of this provision shall be revised to read: In the event this offer is not accepted, or in the event that any conditions hereto are not satisfied, or in the event of a breach of this contract by Seller, and it is understood that the election of Article (c) of Provision 8 is a breach of this contract by Seller, then the earnest money shall be returned to Buyer. Additionally and in the event of such breach Seller is required to reimburse Buyer for all expenses incurred for which Buyer can show receipt, payment will be made upon demand of said receipts, but such return and reimbursement shall not affect any other remedies available to Buyer for such breach.

Amendment to PROVISION 8. INSPECTIONS: The definition of "plumbing" is herein defined to mean and include the complete water and sewerage systems, along with all components, appliances, and fixtures of which said systems rely upon for their proper operation. The definition of "good working order" is herein defined to mean working and in good repair, "good repair" is further defined to mean that no additional repairs should be expected within five (5) years from the date of this contract. In regard to built in appliances or appliances and components necessary to the proper operation of the listed systems in this provision "good repair" will also be extended to include that a useful service period remains of not less than five (5) years. This is to be calculated from manufacturer's useful service life expectations, if so publish-

ed. Inspections are hereby stated to included the structural integrity and condition of the building(s) and its components parts.

Addition to PROVISION 8 and hereby defined as PROVISION 8, ARTICLE (v): Seller is herein asked to reveal and disclose all defects, which be known to him, about and of said building(s), systems, and property.

Addition to PROVISION 8 and hereby defined as PROVISION 8, ARTICLE (vi): Seller is herein asked to reveal any and all hazardous waste and or toxins which may exist upon or under said property. Buyer herein reserves the right to have property inspected for hazardous waste and/or toxins. Disclosure of such material will provide for Buyers election of (a) terminating contract without forfeiture of earnest money, (b) continuation of contract with seller responsible for removal and cleanup as provided by the controlling federal agencies' guidelines, or (c) continuation of contract with buyer responsible for cleanup and removal.

Food For Thought

The amendments above represent only a few of the many things the buyer may find he needs to insert into a contract to protect his interest. Failure to give thought to these provisions and protecting one's rights could prove to be a costly mistake. If any of the amendments listed above represent useful items which you could use in your contracts, feel free to do so. The main idea, though, is to make you aware that a standard contract may not really protect your rights as a buyer. Although a real estate agent or attorney can make suggestions, it is ultimately up to you to make sure your rights and desires are protected and disclosed in the contract. First read it and then make any and all changes you feel prudent. If the seller feels your demands are inappropriate there will be a time and place for negotiations.

HAZARDOUS AND TOXIC WASTE

<u>Toxic wastes present serious dangers to would-be property owners</u>. "Many Americans have lost some or all of their home equity to environmental contamination. Nobody knows how many people are in this fix," said Mary Granfield in *Money Magazine*, "but the number is almost certainly rising as toxic dumps proliferate. Some 40 million Americans live within four miles of the 1,235 sites that have made the U.S. Environmental Protection Agency's Superfund National Priority List - sort of the most wanted list of hazardous waste and about 50 to 100 new sites turn up each year. EPA officials think the toxic tally will eventually reach 2,000 sites, but others expect it to go much higher."

Unfortunately you do not have to live atop a Superfund site to have problems. The waste material that Mary was reporting on in her article concerns 44 homes that were threatened by a methane gas explosion from a decaying scrapwood dump that was discovered under the four-year-old development.

Don't Get Caught In A Dump

It may be impossible to guard completely against being caught in one of the many environmental waste time bombs hidden throughout this land. But there are ways to reduce the odds of it happening to you. Clearly, some places have higher risk factors than others. Some places have risk factors so low that it simply would not be prudent to spend a great deal of money looking for toxic wastes. Other places, however, could warrant spending thousands of dollars to guard against owning a toxic dump.

Remember in the "Intent to Purchase Contract" to add provisions concerning toxic wastes, then decide how much investigation or inspection the property warrants. The following is a list of procedures you can use:

1. Check the water supply, especially if it is from a well or source other than a public utility company.

2. Investigate the surrounding area. Look for anything that might raise a red flag. Pay particular interest to business and industry in the area. Take a drive - take a walk - but take a close look. If you see something that doesn't look right you may have to investigate further or hire someone else to do the job for you.

3. Find out how the property was used in the past. You can hire firms such as environmental management or engineering groups to search county records to trace a 50 to 60 year history of the property. Or you may be able to do this yourself by simply going to the tax office and asking them for a list of past owners. Many county tax offices are now computerized and may be willing to help you with this task. Be on the lookout for any business that might have been involved with radiation, petroleum, or chemicals. An old apple orchard because of the pesticides used, could be cause for alarm. The title search is also an excellent source for finding out who owned the property.

4. Check for radon, a natural radioactive gas being found in the newer and better insulated homes of today. Inexpensive do-it-yourself kits are available for around $50. Make sure it's approved by the EPA or other consumer agency.

5. Have an inspector make a visual inspection for common hazards like lead and asbestos. Consider this especially in older properties. An engineer, architect, or member of the Environmental Assessment Association could make this inspection. Cost is approximately $100 to $300.

6. If you still feel unsafe or unsure, consult an environmental engineer for assistance. Depending on the need and risk factor they can perform many tests and inspections. Cost could range from a few dollars to thousands of dollars.

Important References

Your county health department _____

Your state health department _____

National Testing Laboratories 1 (800) 458-3330

To find who sells the radon test kits call your state radiation office. You can get the number from the EPA's radon hotline, (800) 767-7236. Your State or the EPA can recommend firms that can help you remove any radon that you may find.

The Citizen's Clearinghouse for Hazardous Wastes can send you a neighborhood toxic report to help identify any known hazardous sites in your area. (703) 237-2249.

A new company that has started and may be worth investigating. Per a recent editorial: Starting March 1, 1993, home buyers, sellers or lenders in all 50 states will be able to order by phone comprehensive environmental profiles on any residential address in the U.S. for a flat charge of $75. (800) 989-0402.

For general and/or routine walk-through and visual inspections you can contact the Environmental Assessment Association to find members who have passed the association's environmental exam. The telephone number is (602) 483-8100.

THE TITLE SEARCH

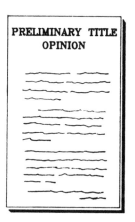

After the buyer signs and presents the owner with the "Intent to Purchase Contract" and decides on what, if any, environmental precautions are needed, the next order of business should be the title search.

A title search presents what is called a *chain of title*. This chain is an examination of all recorded transfers of the property, from the beginning up to the present. It may not necessarily begin at the very first creation of title but it must reference back a number of years. The number of years varies from state to state but averages between 40 to 60 years. In addition the title search will be a summation of events important to the title. Like a real chain, the strength of any one title can be no stronger than its weakest link. If a defective link exists and is discovered, the written title may be void or at least faulty from that point. The title search will probably be done by your attorney, or it may be done by a title abstract company.

HERE IS A TIP THAT MAY HELP: Remember that the person that you are buying the property from probably had to have a title search done for their title insurance. Request, in the intent to purchase contract that a copy of their title search and title insurance be given to you within 10 days of acceptance of the intent to purchase contract. You want to find out who the insurance carrier is because that same company will often provide a discount to renew the policy with them. This is because they will already have most of the title search information, leaving the remainder to be easily updated.

TITLE INSURANCE

As the name implies, "title insurance," is insurance provided by a company to ensure that you are provided with a title clear of all title defects, other than those stated in the policy. For a fee they assume a financial responsibility. The amount of responsibility is, of course, the amount of the policy. The amount of the policy will always be at least equal to the mortgage but should be for the full purchase price. Title policies ordinarily insure against taxes and assessments, bonds, trust deeds, mortgages, easements, liens, forgery, heirs, leases, attachments on the title, and many other items.

However, title policies do not insure against everything. Careful examination will reveal many disclaimers in the policies issued. Unless otherwise stated, a policy is limited to title information of record, not of unrecorded documents. In addition title insurance companies do not normally insure against bankruptcy power, eminent domain, ordinances, and other regulations which might adversely affect the property.

Title companies are in business to take risks. A close examination of almost any title will reveal something that will present an uncertainty. The insurance company, after a study of the title search, bets that those uncertainties will not surface to affect the title and thus provide you with an insurance policy to protect you from that possibility. Without this form of protection, court action might be required to clear even the smallest of defects in the title. This could result in months or even years before titles could be transferred. If the insurance company feels that a defect has a great chance of damaging the title, they will either not insure the property or will write in a disclaimer to protect themselves.

DEEDS AND THEIR PARTS

The final service the attorney will do for the new landowner is to prepare a contract of the property transaction. Where land is the property to be transferred, the contract takes the form of a document called a DEED. A deed to property is a contract. This contract or deed to purchase property is an agreement between two or more parties to transfer title from the seller (GRANTOR) to the buyer (GRANTEE).

The deed is made up of many parts and should represent a summary of the intent of the parties to convey a certain parcel of land. The law stipulates that for this agreement to be valid it must be a written contract. What a deed does is transfer from the Grantor to the Grantee all rights, title, and interest to the property. Nowhere does the deed specifically say that ownership is being transferred. In fact, ownership under the law can be difficult to define.

Many states (but not all) further stipulate that this contract or deed must also be filed with the proper agencies before it can become a valid agreement. The proper recording agency is usually located in the courthouses in those towns designated to conduct the legal affairs of the county. These towns are commonly referred to as the county seats. Within most courthouses the place where the actual deed is stored is called the office of the "Register of Deeds". Some places employ different names such as "Record Room" or "Deed Room."

So, if one wished to find a particular deed he would generally go to the office of the Register of Deeds, located in the courthouse of the county of the state where the property is located. Here you would find volumes of books devoted to storing and recording this vital information. These books are referred to as *Deed Books*. When referencing a particular deed it is customary to refer to it as that deed recorded in *Deed Book 984 at Page 145*. Many times this is simply abbreviated as *D.B. 984 P. 145*.

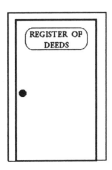

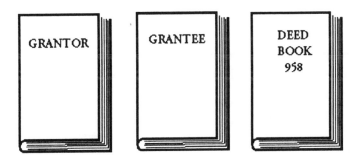

Deed books are usually stored in the Register of Deeds office, which is often located in the courthouse. The Grantor (seller) and the Grantee (buyer) books are the index to the deed books and are in alphabetical order.

EASEMENTS

The recorded deed is to also represent a summary of the property as disclosed from the title search. This should include reference to the chain of title (previous owner[s]) and all deed references. It should also include references to any and all encumbrances upon the property. Encumbrances will primarily include, but are not limited to, EASEMENTS. Additionally the deed should note any EXCEPTIONS to the deed.

Exceptions to the deed could be held by previous owners or could be held in reserve by the grantor himself.

Easements can generally be categorized as being Right-of-Way easements, Utility easements, or Drainage easements. Right-of-Way easements are created to allow someone other than the landowner ingress and egress, to move over and through the property for some purpose.

Utility easements are created to allow utility companies to cross through and on the property to install and maintain the utility. This normally includes water, sewer, gas, electric, telephone, and TV cable. They can be above ground or below ground. They could be minor or major transmission lines.

Drainage easements are created to allow the runoff of rain water from other properties, through other properties, and sometimes to other properties. The process of carrying the water will usually consist of surface ditches but could include underground or above ground methods of transportation. Here again they can be minor or major easements.

UNDERGROUND   GAS   LINE

As our friends here are about to find out, easements can be big trouble !

Easements Cause Big Problems

Of all the problems created from property ownership, easements can take credit for many of them. Easements are often overlooked or simply ignored. Undisclosed and unlocated easements have great capabilities to do harm to the property owner. The title search should be the first defense in disclosing them. The surveyor, if armed with this information, should then be able to locate them. All major easements should be referenced in the deed and preferably referenced by the deed that created them and should be shown on the survey map. Minor easements are not normally referenced in the deed but should be located and shown on the survey map.

Exceptions Leave Something Out

Exceptions to a deed would include portions of the property or rights which the Grantor may have owned or otherwise had, rights to which are not being passed on to the Grantee. This could mean that a portion of the property which he originally purchased is being retained by him or is being transferred to someone else. A right to use an easement for ingress and egress would not necessarily have to be passed on to a new owner if there are other means of ingress to the property. An exclusion of this nature can however, adversely affect a property.

As we see there are many varied reasons and usages for easements and exceptions. For whatever reason all EASEMENTS and EXCEPTIONS should always be referenced in the new deed and should be referenced by the deed that created them. Exceptions to this can be made of some minor easements. However ALL should be shown on the recorded survey map or plat. There are many horror stories of people building homes over easements not discovered. How comfortable would you feel if you found that your home was built over a large natural gas line?

THE LEGAL DESCRIPTION OF YOUR DEED

All parts of the deed are important but topping the list is the deed description. Not only is it one of the most important items of the deed but it is singularly the most abused part of the deed. More trouble, more legal problems, and more grief may have been caused because of poor or dysfunctional legal descriptions than probably any one source or item. The next chapter goes into much greater detail about the legal description but one thing bears repeating. The deed should reference the previous chain of title. The description in the deed in most cases need only be a reference to the recorded survey map. If the recorded survey map is to be recorded with this deed, so much the better. If the referenced survey map is a re-survey and based on a previous recorded map, then the new map should have reference to the previous map and its recording.

The legal description is a written summary created from the survey map of the property. Among attorneys there seem to be two different schools of thought as to the creation of this description. Some attorneys will create a very short description which primarily references the recorded survey map for the details. This is referred to as a "description by reference to a plat or map." Still others will recite almost word for word everything that is on the survey map. This is referred to as a metes and bounds description. Then there are some attorneys who include both the metes and bounds description and the reference to plat and map.

Metes and bounds descriptions can be and often are very lengthy and complicated. The act of trying to put into words alone, that which is shown graphically on a map has resulted in numerous and needless errors. Many of these errors can be attributed to faulty dictation, typing, and copying. The following quotes are from James B. McLaughlin, Jr., co-author of *"North Carolina Boundary Law and Adjoining Landowner Disputes."*

"In today's modern society full of residential developments on a large scale, the use of metes and bounds descriptions is often impracticable and in the opinion of this writer, ill-advised. Therefore, the common practice has developed of describing particular tracts of real estate by referring to a plat or map. This is particularly true in urban areas. This practice of referring to the conveyed land by reference to a plat or map has also resulted in some drafters of deeds (attorneys) using plat and map references <u>and</u> metes and bounds descriptions in the same deed. This is believed to be a poor practice. However, it has happened and will undoubtedly continue to happen. What is the rule for the situation where the reference to the plat conveying, for example, lot 1, block "A" of Divine Shores Subdivision, is inconsistent with the metes and bounds description also contained in the same deed?"

What happens indeed? Unfortunately and seemingly inconsistent with the above quote from a respected attorney, a vast majority of the deeds I review are of the type Mr. McLaughlin refers to as poor practice and ill-advised. But because there are so many of these metes and bounds descriptions being written today I'm including here a list of things they should include if they are in fact done. There will, of course, be some instances when it is necessary to include a metes and bounds description. The following discussion will give some guidelines to their format.

Metes and Bounds Description

If a metes and bounds description is a part of your deed, it should include the bearings and distances which describe the property being conveyed. Adjoining property owners along the property line should be called out and anything of particular importance about the line should be mentioned, for example, *thence N 30 45 E 350.0 feet, along and with the center of a ditch and being bounded by Jim Smith on the West, to an Iron, being the Northwest corner of the property.* A line described in this way provides four important things that define, or could be used to recreate, the property line.

The Beginning

The description should start at the beginning. But there will often be two beginnings. The first point of the beginning should be from a point not on the property but from some publicly known and recognized monument. This monument could be in the form of a United States or State Agency survey system monument or even the center-line-intersection of two public roads. This point will usually be reflected as a tie line on the survey map. Although often referred to as the beginning this point should be referred to as "commencing" rather than beginning, e.g. "commencing at a U.S. Geodetic Monument stamped Base-1, N 32 15' 45" E 578.90 feet to the point of beginning". This would allow for only one beginning and that point should be a part of the property itself.

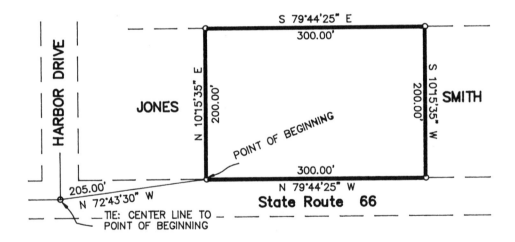

The first point of beginning in this illustration is the tie from the intersection of roads to the second point of beginning which is the true beginning of our property and corner to Jones.

Another Beginning

The second point of beginning normally represents a monument located on the property and being a part of the property. From this second point of beginning, the description will go on to describe the boundaries of the property and then should return to the second point of beginning. In this manner the description closes back on itself and represents a closed figure from which to compute the area, which should also be noted in the legal description.

Because the legal description is a written summary of the survey map, the survey map should always be recorded with the deed or should show reference to where the map is recorded. This is necessary because the written description cannot show everything that is included on the survey map. As the map is in graphic form, it is generally better suited and relied upon, not only to be more detailed but more correct. On more than one occasion typos and/or other errors in the description have resulted in ambiguities in the property boundaries that can be explained or corrected only by examination of the map.

chapter 5

EVALUATING DEEDS
AND SURVEYS

COMPARING GOOD WITH BAD

At the end of this booklet you will find two maps and the deed descriptions written from these maps. One map and its description represent a very good set of documents, the other a very poor set of documents. To illustrate the difference we will analyze the two side by side.

Lay the two maps together and notice the title block. Notice that both maps tell us that the property is located in Township No. 8, Fantasy County, North Carolina. Moving from the title block map "A" tells you that the property is located N 29 05' 27" E 127.8 feet from the center-line-intersection of River Road and Ahoy Road. It further states that the property is N 15 30' 50" E 199.18 feet from an iron found at the right-of-way intersection of these two roads. With these ties from the intersection and iron it should be easy to locate the southwest corner of the property.

The Good Survey

Map "A" has effectively and reasonably shown you where in the USA this property is located and how to find the southwest corner. This southwest corner is the *beginning* of the property and the map gives the various bearings and distances around the property to further define its location. Maps should be read in a clockwise manner from the *beginning* back to the *beginning*.

Notice that iron monuments were found at three corners and two irons were set by the survey. One of the irons found was 1.68 feet off the actual corner and outside the property. This should be important to know so the owner does not build or try to improve his property up to that monument. In the real world it is not uncommon to find an iron out of position in this manner but it should be important to note these discrepancies on the map. The house was drawn on the property and appropriate dimensions given for its location. By dimensioning, the house has now become one large permanent monument.

The map also references two additional irons on the adjoining property. The adjoining property owners with reference to their *Deed Book and Page* or the lots (in the case of a subdivision) are shown. On the call from the right-of-way of the two roads to our *beginning*, the deed or subdivision map calls for 200.00 feet but this survey only found 199.18 feet between the irons found. Fortunately the surveyor in this instance has provided us with a probable clue for this discrepancy. The definition from the center-line of Ahoy Road is 25.8 feet when it should be 25.0 feet. This would at least suggest that the iron at the right-of-way is 0.8 feet into the property of Lot 27. If it were not possible to show why this discrepancy occurred we would be forced to show a deed overlap of the 0.8 feet.

A discrepancy was also found in the tie between Lot 28 and Lot 26. The deed calls for 100.00 feet between the irons but this survey found 100.21 feet. The survey did not try to find the reason for this difference even though it creates a small void between the properties. A small void in this manner is not nearly as significant as an overlap. The surveyor would probably need to survey several additional lots to find the reason and this could needlessly drive up the cost of the survey.

The fence on the north lines of Lot 28 is shown to be on the property line and does not encroach into the lot. This is important because if the fence beside the cemetery were old and did encroach it could represent a real problem with these property lines. Be wary of old fences, hedges, and ditches as they can be clues to deed discrepancies, adverse, or acquiescent property.

The location map is helpful by relating our site, River Road, and Ahoy Road with a major road such as U. S. 819. Because Ahoy Road is a loop road a second site is possible, as there are two intersections of River and Ahoy roads. The location map makes clear where the real site is located.

Two additional important things this map does is reference the current *deed book* and *page number* for the property that is shown on the map. The map also references a previous survey map. This reference should be a reference to the original survey or deed that created this particular piece of property. It is very important that references are included on the survey map to provide a link to the chain of title and original survey.

Map "A" contains the basic information necessary for a survey. Each state may require more or additional things but NEVER should any map show less than what is provided and shown on map "A". A tie to a "geodetic" monument would be a great complement to this survey; however a geodetic monument may not be available to each and every property surveyed. Every state will have its own requirements, but for most the requirement is that if property surveyed is within 2,000 feet of a geodetic monument, a tie to that monument must be shown on the survey map.

The Bad Survey

After examining Map "A", I'm sure you will immediately notice many deficiencies with Map "B". First this map does tell us the property is located in Fantasy County, North Carolina. It does not give us a tie from the intersection of River and Ahoy Roads but it does give us a 100.00 foot tie to the right-of-way lines of these two roads, but as we have already seen from map "A" there is a problem of 0.8 of a foot with this tie.

The distance of 100.00 feet matches exactly what the subdivision map or deed description calls for, but it does not tell us what if anything was found at the corner. I have seen many instances where calls such as this were written on a map to show merely what the distance or bearing is supposed to be, not what it actually surveys in the field to be. Such practices are worthless as it is the survey's function to physically locate and report accurately the field survey findings. Be wary of any map that shows no differences from what is called for in the deeds. The map may be correct but it is rare that monuments exist exactly in the position they should. In a resurvey of even a four corner lot I would expect to find at least one or two monuments missing the corner by a couple of inches. The is common and within the tolerance of error of todays surveys. The only real error is hiding and not showing these differences on the survey map.

Recall from map "A" that if that distance is from the iron found at the corner of River and Ahoy Road, then the fence will now be encroaching. Of course, this survey does not show us what the point is or where the fence is located, so we have no real way of knowing what the true situation is.

As we proceed from the *beginning* of this lot we discover that the map contains the exact same bearings and distances as did Map "A". Correctly, these bearings and distances are the same as the deed description calls for. However, this map does not reveal what evidence if any was found to support the conclusion of the survey. Not one of the corners is marked or identified. If we are to presume that irons were found at each corner then we must also assume that all these irons were exactly on the corner as they should be. This would in fact be a very rare occurrence in the real world.

This survey does not show us what was found at the corners nor does it reveal if any of the missing irons were reset. The fence is not shown nor is the encroaching shed. The only thing this survey reveals that would be different from the original subdivision map or deed is that there is now a house on the lot. This information is of little value since dimensions are not supplied from the house to the property lines.

Map "B" is obviously inferior to Map "A" and leaves out some very important information. In fact we learn little from this survey that would not be disclosed by examining the original subdivision map or deed description. Map "B" does not even provide us a location map so we are left to wonder if the site is at the first or second intersection of River and Ahoy Roads.

Basics Of The Survey

The basic function of a survey is to first locate the correct property to be surveyed, and then to locate the monuments and any other evidence that witnesses the property's existence. To locate the correct property the surveyor must have maps and deeds telling him how to get to the property and what he should be looking for.

Land surveying is described as a profession of art and science. The science involves measuring and calculating angles and distances. The science of surveying can be taught and learned by many. It is the art of surveying that is not so easily learned. The art of surveying involves bring together the angles and distances gathered in the field to form the best possible solution to support the geometry of the property called for in the deed. Here is a good example of how difficult this is. Place your left hand one foot in front of your face, fingers spread. Assume this to be the property called for in the deed. Now place your right hand directly over your left, palm to palm. If all things were perfect you should be able to adjust your right hand so that the left hand is directly behind and hidden by your right hand. Assume the right hand is the information gathered by a field survey of the property. At some places you will continue to see portions of your left hand. You can only adjust and shift your hands to make the best fit but you cannot make the right hand fit exactly over the left. After you have made the best fit you possibly can, keep your hands together and twist them around to look from the other side. Do they still fit or do you need to do more adjusting? Fitting a deed description and the field information is much like the procedure you have just gone through with your hands. How well the surveyor is able to perform this art of surveying is what distinguishes him from those that merely measure. It is this fitting of the written deed with what actually exist in the real world that causes discrepancies.

Discrepancies Between The Deed and the Survey

The procedure you have gone through with your hands should help you to understand why there is discrepancies between the deed and the field survey. A more specific example of how these discrepancies arise can be show in the following example: Suppose a legal description starts thus; Beginning at an iron pipe the Southwest corner, thence N 30 45' 30" W 385.5 feet to the Northwest corner, thence... In this portion of the description the NW corner of the property is defined only by following the bearing and distance listed. A surveyor in his field work might find that by following the above course he ends up 10 feet from a monument that appears to be honored by the property owners. Thus a dilemma is created. Is the bearing and distance wrong or is the monument wrong? Many factors would need to be evaluated to decide which is correct. In this instance we will assume that the surveyor has no better information available and is therefore bound to honor the bearing and distances given in the deed description which may, in fact, create a void or overlap of 10 feet between the property owners.

If in the above example the deed description read: Beginning at an iron pipe the Southwest corner, thence N 30 45' 30" W 385.5 feet to the Northwest corner, an iron pipe. In this version the wording which includes the "iron pipe" as the corner makes quite a difference. If it can be verified to be the iron pipe mentioned in the deed, the line could be run from iron pipe to iron pipe. The bearing and distances would be assigned less weight in establishing the corner.

There are no hard and fast rules for deciding these discrepancies. Each must be solved individually by closely examining the wording of the deeds and the physical evidence found. This is only one example of how a poorly worded "description" causes problems for property owners.

The Survey Provides No Legal Right.

The survey does not give any legal grounds or claim to the property; it merely reports what evidence exists on the ground to support your claim to a certain parcel of property as described by your deed. The recorded deed is your written claim to a parcel, portion, lot, or tract of property. The monuments which exist on the ground are the only physical evidence available to support the deed and ultimately your claim to the property. The loss of any or all of these monuments can and does make reestablishing the exact location of your deed not only difficult but sometimes impossible. To understand this is to understand the importance of preserving the monuments at your property corners. In Chapter Six, we will show you some effective and economical ways to preserve, protect, and document this valuable evidence.

All the surveyor's results of the property survey should be shown and accurately reflected on the survey map and should provide the basic information required by every state's code of minimum standards of practice. If you should have a survey done and any of the above items are not included on your map, talk with the person responsible and ask that they be included or get a reasonable explanation as to why they should not be included. Keep in mind that a great deal of work goes into a survey map and honest unintentional errors do happen from time to time, in which case you should find most surveyors eager to correct any error.

COMPARING THE LEGAL DESCRIPTIONS

As with the survey maps "A" and "B" we will compare the legal descriptions for these two properties. As the legal description incorporates components of the survey and title search, its quality is dependent on both. Obviously the legal description of "B" will not be as good as that of "A" because of the difference in quality of the survey, reasons we have already discussed. But the description does more than just duplicate the map bearings and distances from the survey.

The legal description should provide reference to the chain of title. This chain could be merely a reference to the previous owner's deed book and page. If the previous deed book was not complete, then additional deed references may be necessary to complete the new title. Having a deed with a broken chain of title is not uncommon as many earlier deeds thought to be complete in their time are found not to be so today. Many of these deficiencies are discovered through examination of the title search.

All exceptions, easements, and right-of-ways should be noted in the legal description. These things can also be discovered through the title search which is another very good reason for having the title search done and given to the surveyor. Then he may be able to locate the exceptions, easements, and right-of-ways and delineate them on his map.

The best example of what we consider a proper deed description, requires that we simply reference the map or plat for that description. Examination of Deed "A" will reveal that the map is referenced, along with the previous deed. In most instances this should be all that is required of the description. No attempt has been made in this deed to summarize the survey map or copy the previous deed which, of course eliminates many needless errors which are often introduced by trying to create a metes and bounds description from a survey map.

On map "A" we have shown an easement for a natural-gas line through the property. Easements and their placement can and do have a detrimental effect on the value and suitability of properties. Know what they are and where they are. Not only should easements be shown on a survey map but they should also be called out in the legal description with the deed references which created them.

In the case of Map "B" we have presumed that the title search was not supplied to the surveyor and that through his normal and restrictive deed research the easement was not discovered. If the attorney preparing the deed were to base his legal description solely on this survey and did an inadequate title search then the gas line would be left to the present or future owner to discover. It becomes painfully evident that a few careless omissions or errors can be cause for future problems or even catastrophes. Unfortunate, these types of errors have been committed many times in the past and continue to be committed today.

To illustrate the problem that occurs from creating a metes and bounds description, in the legal description of Map "B", we have made an error that is commonly found in descriptions of this type. Can you find it?

The error can be found by examining the bearing of N 78 21' 21" E found in the legal description. The correct bearing as shown on the map should be S 78 21' 21" E. This seems a minor error of only one letter. However that one letter moves the line over 43.04 feet north for every 100 feet of length of the line. In this case it moves the corner out of position by over 59.21 feet. One small letter can make a large error.

Close examination of the two deed descriptions will reveal the differences, strengths, and weakness of the two descriptions. Again if you find problems with a deed written for you, talk with the person responsible and request that they correct any errors, omissions, or other problems.

THE SURVEY CHECKLIST

To evaluate your survey map, have a copy of your title search, a copy of the previous deed, and a previous map if available. Then answer these questions:

_____ Does the map guide you or a stranger to the property?

_____ Does the map show what evidence (monuments) were found to support the survey?

_____ Does the map show ties to monuments not found exactly on the property corners?

_____ Does the map show ties to monuments on adjoining properties?

_____ Does the map show at least one tie to a permanent and publicly recognized benchmark or landmark? Example: U.S. or State Geodetic Monument, or center-line intersection of roads?

_____ Does the new survey conform to or differ from the previous legal description and/or survey map?

_____ Is the current or previous legal description referenced?

_____ Is the previous map or plat referenced?

_____ Is reference made to deed book and page numbers of adjoining property owners? In the case of subdivisions, are the book and page for the recorded map shown?

_____ Are there EASEMENTS OR EXCEPTIONS in the title search that should be located and shown on the map?

_____ Are all easements and right-of-ways shown?

_____ Is the total area shown?

_____ Are all structures shown and dimensioned to the property lines?

_____ The map should note if the property falls in or out of any flood hazard areas referenced and delineated by the Federal FIRM (Flood Insurance Rate Map).

THE RECORDED DEED CHECKLIST

To evaluate your deed, you should have a copy of your title search, a previous deed, and the survey map.

_____ Check and proof read for correct spelling of names. Is the name correct for everyone to be listed as owner(s) included as grantee? This is important if you wish to include your wife, husband, or others.

_____ Are the previous deed references and maps noted?

_____ Compare the new legal description with the legal description of the previous deed. Are they the same? If not, does the new description explain the reason for the differences? It should, and should show other deed references as explanation.

_____ Are all exceptions to and from the original deed referenced?

_____ Are all right-of-ways and easements found in the title search or from the survey map referenced? Exception to this may be made with minor drainage easements.

The following would be needed only if the description creates a metes and bounds description.

_____ The deed description should begin at the same place the survey map begins, as explained previously.

_____ Compare the new legal description with the survey map. If the legal description does attempt to recite the bearings and distances from the survey map of the property lines, it should do so exactly. Many problems have arisen because of typographic errors such as a bearing being labeled Southeast when it should be Southwest. Proof read carefully.

_____ Just as the survey shows what evidence was found at the corners of the property, so too should the legal description recite this information. Example, beginning at a Concrete Monument... to an Iron Pipe.

_____ Total area from the survey should be included in the legal description.

ONE FINAL WORD ABOUT
YOUR DEED RECORDINGS

Today when you purchase property you will probably be required by your lending institution to have a survey. The survey protects your investment as well as theirs. There is a trend, especially in subdivision lots, not to record the survey with the deed. I fail to understand the rationale for this and believe it provides no benefit to the property owner.

I must presume the reason for not recording the map is that it is a re-survey and not the original survey which created the property? It is certainly important to have the reference to the original survey. But it seems equally important to show what evidence exists today to support that original survey. A comparison of a re-survey with an original survey will generally show many additions and changes. Are these not important? Certainly they are important. If a re-survey does its job properly it shows reference to the original survey map. If the re-survey map is recorded with the deed, then both maps are made a part of the deed by reference. This could only enhance the value of the deed.

The small additional fee required to record the map with the deed, makes this practice of recording the map worthwhile. The banks and insurance companies understand the importance of a survey; they are going to require you to have one. Make the survey that you've paid for work for you.

**REQUEST THAT THE
SURVEY MAP BE RECORDED
WITH YOUR DEED.**

chapter 6

YOUR "MARKS" FOR ALL TO SEE

In this chapter we will discuss actual methods that the landowner can use to preserve the property corner monument or position of the property corner. To do so we must first look at making the property corner monument more permanent. Then we can look at adding accessories to the property corner that will aid in reproducing the position the monument occupied should it become lost or destroyed.

MAKE IT PERMANENT

Most of the property corners set today are either iron pipes or iron re-bars. They are used because they are plentiful and easily found by metal detectors. The metal detector is the single most effective instrument available to the surveyor for locating these iron pipes or re-bars. Concrete monuments are used but not as frequently as the iron pipes because of the time and expense. For the surveyor an iron pipe can be driven in the ground in a fraction of the time it takes to set a concrete monument.

Concrete monuments seem to last and take on a special significance to the surveyor retracing a property boundary. Because the concrete monument is used so sparingly and has a more lasting value, the surveyor often suspects that concrete monuments were placed with more care than is normally taken with iron pipes. The surveyor is often more hesitant to question the correctness of concrete monuments than he is of an iron pin. And well he should be because the iron pin is easily moved and subject to damage and vandalism. The concrete monument requires considerably more effort to dislodge or remove.

Better Monuments

Most properties have iron pins at their property corners. But with a minimal amount of effort we can turn these monuments into concrete monuments and gain more permanent and respected corners. Few tools and materials are needed and the expense and time are negligible.

We want to create these concrete monuments only where we have iron pins in good repair and in their proper location. Very simply the easiest thing to do is dig a hole around the present iron and pour concrete in the hole and around the iron pin. The simplest method of digging the hole is with post hole diggers or with a small spade shovel. As all this activity of digging is sure to dislodge the iron we must take precautions to insure its proper location once we are done.

Reference Stakes

Before we begin our digging activities it is necessary to set some temporary wooden stakes. These stakes are used to insure that the iron gets back to its original position even if we have to remove it temporarily. The illustrations that follow will show how to arrange the stakes and make the necessary measurements.

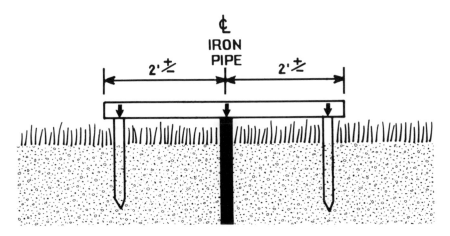

Cut-away showing placement of wooden stakes and reference board on top. Make marks on the stakes and reference board so the iron can be replaced in its exact location. Care must be taken not to knock the wood stakes out of position during construction.

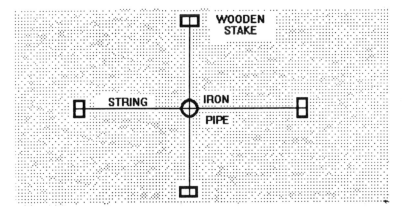

Aerial view showing an alternate method to the above illustration using four stakes and string. After getting the string in position and marked on the stakes, the string can be removed to work around the iron and then replaced when resetting the iron.

Once the temporary stakes are set we can begin digging. Ideally, we will want to dig a hole about 6 to 8 inches in diameter around the iron. And we want our hole to be about 12 to 18 inches deep. Again the post hole digger or spade shovel will be the best tool for this task. As the digging begins we may start out with the iron in place. Getting deeper with our hole the iron will probably become dislodged and may be removed to permit easier digging. Don't worry, that's why we placed the stakes.

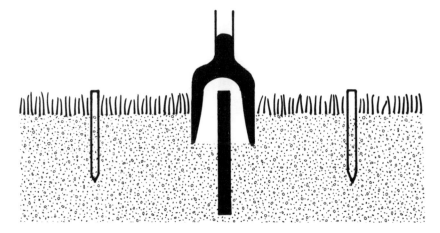

These illustrations show digging around the iron with a spade shovel and post hole digger. The spade shovel or post hole digger can both be used and are well suited to the task. The hole should be at least 12 to 18 inches deep.

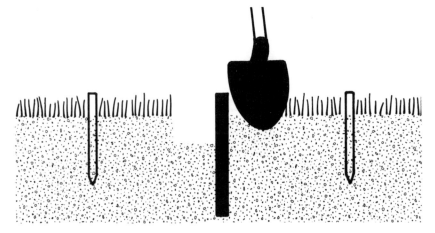

After the hole has been dug to the proper depth we can then proceed to fill it with concrete. In today's world of instant gravy and mashed potatoes we are fortunate to be able to purchase instant concrete from almost any lumber yard. One bag can probably fill several holes. There is no need to mix the mixture with water before putting it in the hole. Simply pour the dry mixture from the bag directly into the hole and then add water. Although this does not make the strongest form of concrete it will be adequate for our purposes.

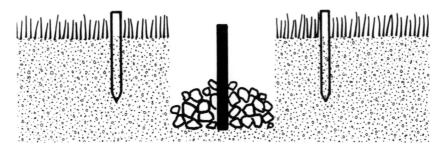

After our hole is dug we can place stones around the bottom of the iron to stabilize it and save concrete.

After the concrete has been poured and before it has a chance to set up we must place the iron pin in the mixture so the concrete can harden around it. If you plan on filling the hole with stones before pouring the concrete, you should place the stones around the iron first and then pour the concrete.

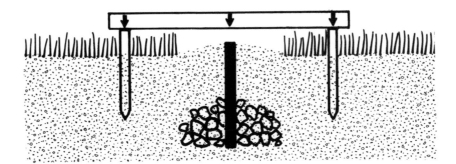

This illustration shows the hole filled with concrete. A small trowel can be used to shape the top of the concrete so water will drain to the outside. Before the concrete cures, replace the reference board and make adjustments to the position of the iron.

After the iron is in the hole, you may have to make slight adjustments to the top of the iron to insure that it gets back to its original position. Using the stakes that we set in the beginning you can easily move the iron around with gentle taps from a hammer before the concrete cures. You may want the iron to protrude above the concrete but if it's in an area subject to yard maintenance, do not make it so high that it could get caught in a lawn-mower blade. A half inch above the concrete, which should be at ground level, should be sufficient. If the iron you are working with is a pipe and open at the top you may want to fill the pipe with concrete so water cannot enter.

Congratulations. If you finished this simple task you have completed the single most important thing you could do to add permanence to your property corners. If you encouraged your neighbor to help with the project both you and he will be fully aware of the corner locations. This in itself can help deter any future problems and misunderstandings about the location of your property lines.

Not all property corners can be given this degree of permanence. And some corners, because of their location, will still be subject to destruction. For such corners accessories can be added to insure that even in the event the corner is lost, its position can easily be established when needed.

CORNER WITNESS MARKERS

In the early days of land development and surveying, additional markers or monuments were often placed near the actual corner monument. The sole function of these additional markers was to provide an alternate means of establishing and replacing the corner monument should it be lost or destroyed. These were and still are referred to as "witness markers." Over the years the practice of placing witness markers near the corner monuments by surveyors has decreased for various reasons.

The rising cost of surveys today increases the need of having a method to replace corners without having to hire a surveyor every time a corner is destroyed. At least one large timber company has reverted to this practice of placing witness markers at their existing property corners. Fortunately we, the property owners, can also place and use these witness markers and make and record the necessary measurements ourselves. Having done this, we can use the witness markers and measurements to replace the corner ourselves.

Witness Monuments Are Versatile

A corner monument can be placed in only one specific spot, and that is, of course, where the property lines meet. Because the corner monument is restricted to an exact location, they often fall in areas that render them extremely vulnerable to being destroyed or lost. We are not so constricted in placing our corner witness markers. In fact we can place them in any desirable location. The only limitation is that we must be able to measure the distance, in a straight line, between the corner monument and witness marker.

A straight line here means that there must not be anything between the two monuments which would interfere with obtaining a direct measurement. The Land Surveyor is confined to measuring or converting all measurements to horizontal. We, in placing and taking our measurements, are not limited to horizontal measurement but should try to adhere, when possible, to the horizontal rather than slope measurement. The illustrations that follow will provide a more graphic representation of the difference between horizontal and slope measurements.

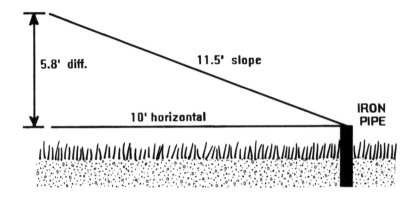

This illustration shows the different measurements that can be obtained using slope verses horizontal measurements. Try to use measurements that are horizontal if possible. If it is not possible using a slope measurement that notes the difference from horizontal will be acceptable, ex. 11.5' slope approximately 6' above horizontal.

CORNER WITNESS SYSTEM

To make corner witness markers useful to the property owner we must establish a procedure and program so the owner can set and utilize these markers for his own benefit. For simplicity we will call these procedures the Corner Witness System.

Triangulation

The corner witness system, as defined here, relies on the mathematical principle of triangulation. Triangulation is a very simple procedure that requires three (3) known points measured to a fourth (4) known point. For our purposes, we will let the three points of the triangle be the witness markers and the fourth point be the corner monument. Triangulating the distances from three points or witness markers, provides one and only one solution for the position of the fourth point, our corner monument. Because only the distances need be known, the skill and tools needed will be minimal.

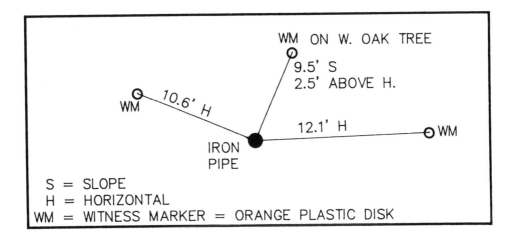

Illustration showing three witness markers and their measurements to an iron pipe. Note that two measurements are horizontal with one placed at a slope distance of 9.5', 2.5' above horizontal.

Placing The Markers

That's the basic concept concerning witness markers. All that remains is to physically place three witness markers in close proximity to your corner monument and record the distances. Simply select three safe sites a convenient distance from the corner and place the witness markers. We recommend that distances from the corner be less than 25 feet; in most cases, 3 to 10 feet will represent more convenient distances. After placing the witness markers, measure and record the distances. The insert provided with this booklet shows a suitable example of recording method and form. Additionally, a blank form is provided for you to copy and use for this purpose.

A Measuring Stick

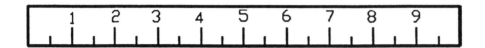

One item we're going to suggest is a straight 10 foot long stick. This can be any dimension from a 2 x 4 to a 1 x 2 furring strip. We can use this stick to help us make horizontal measurements. A survey crew would use the tape measure and plumb bob to make these measurements. But without practice many will find it difficult to stretch a tape out horizontally and measure the tape at the point the plumb bob string crosses the tape while the plumb-bob is directly over the object to be measured. You will need a steady hand and will wish you had a couple extra. Do not be discouraged; we will show you an easier method by substituting the 10 foot stick for the tape measure in some of the illustrations that follow. If the property is level and smooth we need not worry about using these methods to get horizontal measurements, as we can measure by laying the tape directly on the ground.

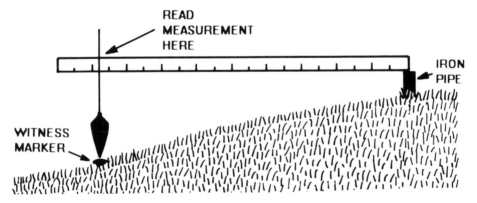

This illustration shows one of several methods that can be employed to make horizontal measurements. This illustration uses a plum bob to mark the reading on the wooden stick where the next illustration uses a carpenter's level. A cloth or steel tape could be substituted for the wooden stick.

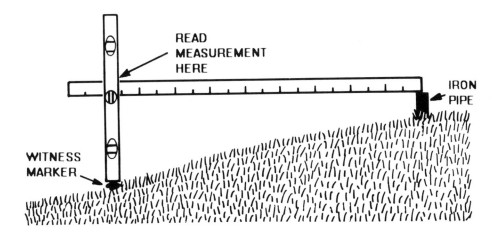

This illustration differs from the previous illustration by substituting a carpenter's level in place of the plum bob. The carpenter's level will be much easier for most people to use that the plum bob.

Here's an alternative to the above method of placing the witness markers if the site is suitable. Preselect the distances you wish to place the witness markers from the corner monument. Let's use, for example, 6 feet. Measure 6 feet from the corner to the site where you wish to place the first witness. Having set the first witness continue in the same method with the second and the third witness until all three are placed a convenient 6 feet from the corner. Now your recording of the distances is greatly simplified.

You are not limited to using either of the above methods. In fact the site will more often dictate which method to use and will sometimes require a combination of the two. You are limited however to placing the witness markers on your own property unless your adjoining owner also participates in this endeavor or grants you permission to use his property for this purpose. This is good reason to involve him in this process, but it is not the only reason. If he will participate, four hands are always better than two. You can share in the expense and lessen the time required.

An even better reason for seeking his assistance is that both you and he will be aware of where the property corner is located and will be demonstrating approval of that location.

Materials

It is very important that the witness markers you place do not become confused with or mistaken for the actual corner monument. What may seem obvious at the time could become confusing as years pass. For that reason we are making available a source to the inexpensive plastic discs intended to be used as witness markers. They are highly visible and engraved with the wording, "**WITNESS MARKER**", "**DO NOT DISTURB**". It is recommended that you do use these or something similarly suitable for the witness markers.

On the last page of this booklet you will find an order form for these disks and other products which may be useful. Of particular interest may be the stakes that are designed to be used with the disk. The stake and disk combination represent what we consider the most convenient and economical materials for those who may be limited to the amount of time they wish to invest. The stakes are nothing more than large nails or spikes that can possible be bought at your local hardware store. We make them available for convenience but with the postage it may be cheaper to buy them locally. You may not even need them at all, many creative people can devise suitable and practical replacements. And we encourage them to do so where practical.. Suggestions for alternatives are provided on the next page. Caution is advised in substituting for the disks with something not suited for their intended purpose. Their expense is small and could save much confusion and cost in the future.

Suggestions For Stake Substitutes

Here are some practical ways to attach the witness disk without going to a lot of expense:

- Dig a small diameter hole, fill with concrete and mount the witness disk at the top.

- Drive an iron pipe in the ground, fill with concrete, waterproof epoxy or other suitable filler with a witness disk on top. A wooden plug or even a wad of paper could be inserted or driven into pipe to save on filler material.

- A disk can be nailed to a tree with a brass nail, eliminating the need for stakes. A disk can be nailed into asphalt, eliminating the need for a stake.

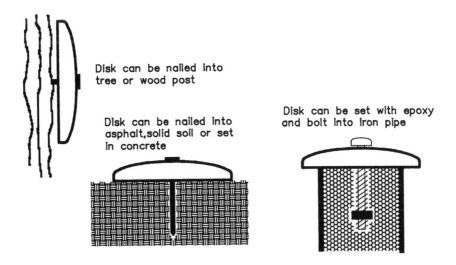

Disk can be nailed into tree or wood post

Disk can be nailed into asphalt, solid soil or set in concrete

Disk can be set with epoxy and bolt into iron pipe

These are but a few of the ways the witness disks can be set. Caution is advised when placing nails in trees that may someday be cut for lumber, a nail can diminish the value of the tree.

Common Tools Needed

Regardless of the materials used for the witness stakes, a few common tools will be required. A hammer will be required to drive the stakes or nails. A 25-foot tape measure will be needed to measure distances. A plumb bob will be needed unless the ground is flat. If you do not own a plum bob, an inexpensive carpenter's plumb bob can be purchased from most hardware stores. However, a carpenter's 3-foot level can often be substituted for the plum bob. You will need to record the distances so pencil and paper will be needed. Included with this book is a blank form that is suitable for the recording of this information. We suggest you make copies of this form to use.

Legal Considerations

If you find that a corner monument is in need of repair or replacement, you should not initiate those repairs without the consent of the adjoining owners. The corner monuments should be considered to be held in joint ownership among all the property owners bounded by the monument. Many states have laws protecting monuments from being removed or damaged. I do not believe these laws would restrict property owners from maintaining or replacing monuments in disrepair or replacing them with more suitable materials, should ALL the property owners agree. However, I do not believe it prudent to do these things without a unanimous decision. If a decision by all can not be reached, then I would suggest hiring a surveyor to perform such work, as they are entrusted with maintaining these corners.

By all means, discuss with and encourage your adjoining property owners to engage in this activity. You will probably find that they share your concerns and by joining together you will not only add lasting value and peace of mind but cement a more permanent and lasting friendship. Do this while your corners are still in place and there is agreement on their correctness. Remember property disputes are not born because people know where their lines are; they arise as a result of not knowing where the lines are.

Finding Your Monuments

Most people know where their property corners are or they know approximately where they should be. If you do not then you will need to find them before you can place witness markers. If you know where one monument is you can measure the distance called for on the map to find the next. Good detective work should help you locate your monuments. In wooded areas most monuments are left protruding from the ground several inches. In areas that are subject to yard maintenance or other activities, the monuments may be at ground level or below. Almost all monuments contain metal, making them easy to locate with a metal detector. This is the reason most monuments are iron pipes or steel re-bars. When a concrete monument is used it must contain some form of metal or cap made of metal. If you are trying to locate monuments, a metal detector may be a necessity.

If you cannot find your monuments you may need the services of a surveyor to locate or reset them. If this is needed be sure to place witness markers soon after the surveyor has marked the corners so you do not have this problem again. For those who do not have the time or ability to undergo these activities, you may wish to hire a survey company to do the work for you.

You may want to place witness markers at all your corners or only at those corners that are in areas subject to abuse and destruction. In the following illustration you will find an example of a form used to sketch and record the information about a particular corner with witness markers.

CORNER WITNESS MARKER RECORDING FORM

OWNER _Michael D. Ryan_   DATE: _3-5-92_
PROPERTY DISC _10.3 AC. TRACT, TAZWELL CO., VA._
DEED BOOK _679_   PAGE _413_   TAX ID # _8-132_
CORNER DESCRIPTION _SOUTHWEST CORNER_

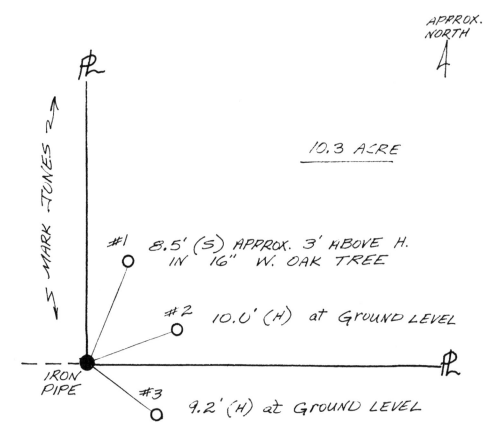

APPROX. NORTH

10.3 ACRE

S MARK JONES

#1   8.5' (S) APPROX. 3' ABOVE H. IN 16" W. OAK TREE

#2   10.0' (H) at GROUND LEVEL

IRON PIPE

#3   9.2' (H) at GROUND LEVEL

SEC. STATE RTE 714

○ = WITNESS MARKER = ORANGE DISK
(S) = SLOPE DISTANCE
(H) = HORIZONTAL DISTANCE

Appendix A

GLOSSARY OF SURVEYING AND ASSOCIATED TERMS

ABSTRACT OF TITLE - A summary of all conveyances, such as deeds, or wills, and legal proceedings, giving the names of the parties, the description of the land, and the agreements, arranged to show the continuity of ownership.

ABUTTER - An owner or occupant whose property adjoins or touches other land.

ACCESSORIES TO CORNERS (USPLS) - Physical objects adjacent to corners to which such corners are referred for their future identification or restoration. Accessories include bearing trees, mounds, pits, ledges, rocks, and other natural features to which distances or directions, or both, from the corner or monument are known, Such accessories are actually a part of the monument.

ACQUIESCENCE - Some act of concurrence by the adjoining owners bearing on the practical location of their common boundary, where the definite, or more accurate position of the line, or lines has not, or cannot be defined by survey, or with the tacit consent of one by interposing a formal objection to what might be an encroachment by the other, all subject to judicial review as to the legal effect.

ADJACENT - Lying near or close to; sometimes, contiguous; neighboring. Adjacent implies that the two objects are not widely separated, though they may not actually touch, while adjoining imports that they are so joined or united to each other that no third object intervenes.

ADJOINING - To lie contiguous to; to be in contact with; to abut upon; sometimes inaccurately, to be near, or in proximity to.

ADVERSE POSSESSION - A method of acquisition of title by possession for a statutory period under certain conditions. It has been described as the statutory method of acquiring title to land by limitation. The possession must be actual; adverse; under claim of right; continuous, open, notorious; exclusive; and hostile. Although color of title is not essential, it is of great evidentiary value in establishing adverse possession. Adverse possession depends on intent of occupant to claim and hold real property in opposition to all the world; and also embodies the idea that owner of, or persons interested in, property have knowledge of the assertion of ownership by the occupant. Payment of taxes alone is not sufficient in itself to establish adverse possesion. It is mandatory that the element of continuous possession exist for the full statutory period.

AGREEMENT - A concurrence between adjoining land owners on the location of their common boundaries, defined in the exercise of good judgement by the parties to the stipulations as needed for interpretation by disinterested persons, including one qualified in land surveying, and as ordinarily required in a deed, subject to judicial opinion in the event of ambiguity or controversy.

ANGLE, HORIZONTAL - An angle in a horizontal plane. The directions may be to objects in the horizontal plane; or they may be the lines of intersection of the horizontal plane with the vertical planes containing the objects.

APPURTENANCE - That which belongs to another thing as principal and passing as incident to it, as a right of way or other easement to land a right of common to pasture, an outhouse, barn, garden or orchard. In a strict legal sense, land cannot pass as an appurtenance to land.

ARBITRATION (land ownership) - The submission for determination of disputed matter to private unofficial persons selected in manner provided by law or agreement. Compulsory arbitration is that which occurs when the consent of one of the parties is enforced by statutory provisions. Voluntary arbitration is by mutual and free consent of the parties. The submission is an agreement by which parties agree to submit their differences to the decision of a referee or arbitrators. It is sometimes termed a reference.

BEARING - The direction of one point or object, with respect to another, where the direction of the line is expressed by the acute angle with respect to a reference meridian. The reference direction can be North or South and the meridian may be assumed, grid, magnetic, astronomic, or geodetic. Typical bearings are N 60 10' E, S 31 17' W, N 17 22' W.

BEGINNING, POINT OF - In metes and bounds descriptions the first point on the boundary of the property being described. After passing through the successive courses the description returns "to the point of beginning." When descriptions start at a reference point not contiguous to the boundary being described, the point of commencing should be used.

BENCH MARK - A relatively permanent material object, natural or artificial, bearing a marked point whose elevation above or below an adopted datum is known. Usually designated as a B.M., such a mark is sometimes qualified as a P.B.M (permanent bench mark) to distinguish it from a T.B.M. (temporary or supplementary bench mark) which is a mark of less permanent character intended to serve for only a comparatively short period of time.

BOUNDARY MONUMENT - A material object placed on or near a boundary line to preserve and identify the location of the boundary line on the ground. Where it is impracticable to establish a monument on or very close to a boundary line, the position of the boundary line on the ground is preserved by reference marks. The term monument is sometimes used to include both the mark on the boundary line and the reference mark.

CERTIFICATE OF TITLE 1)- A document usually given to a home buyer with the deed, stating that the title to their property is clear. It is usually prepared by an attorney or qualified person who has examined the abstract of title for the property. It is only an opinion that title is good; not to be confused with title insurance. 2) A certificate issued to show title registered on Torrens title lands.

CHAIN OF TITLE - A chronological list of documents which comprise the record history of title of a specific parcel of real estate.

CLAIM, - A right or title; challenge of property or ownership of a thing which is wrongfully withheld; means by or through which claimant obtains possession or enjoyment of privilege or thing; under land laws, tract of land taken up by a preemptioner or other settler (and also his possession of it).

COMMENCING, POINT OF - In metes and bounds description, the starting point if not a part of the tract being described, e.g., "commencing at the northwest corner of Section 12, T 112 N, R 17 W; thence southerly along the west line of said section 500 feet to the point of beginning.

CONTROL, CADASTRAL (USPLS) - Lines established and marked on the ground by suitable monuments, which are used as starting and closing points in surveys of the public domain of the United States. The primary control of the public land surveys of the United States consists of base lines, standard parallels (correction lines), principal meridians, and guide meridians.

CONVEYANCE - A written instrument which passes an interest in real property from one person to another; may be a deed, mortgage, lease, but not a will

COURSE - 1) (Land surveying) The bearing of a line; also the bearing and length of a line. 2) (Transit traverse) The azimuth and length of a line, considered together. 4) (Geography) A route on the earth along which a river flows; the river itself.

DATUM, NORTH AMERICAN, 1927 (1927 NAD) - This datum is identical with the North American datum at station Meades Ranch, except that the azimuth, Meades Ranch to Waldo was changed to 75 28' O9.64. It was adopted in 1827 after a readjustment of the triangulation of the entire country in which Laplace azimuths were introduced. It is now the standard geodetic datum on the North American continent.

DEDICATION - To dedicate means to appropriate and set apart land from one's private property to some public use. The dedication may be either express or implied. It is express when there is an express manifestation on the part of the owner of his purpose to devote the land to a particular public use, such as the streets in platted subdivisions. It is implied when the owner's acts and conduct manifest an intention to devote the land to the public use. To make the dedication complete, there must not only be an intention on part of the owner to set apart land for the use and benefit of the public, but there must be an acceptance by the public.

DEED - An instrument in writing which, when executed and delivered, conveys and estate in real property or interest therein.

DEED, GENERAL WARRANTY - A deed in which the grantor warrants the title against defects arising at any time, either before or after the grantor became connected with the land.

DEED, SPECIAL WARRANTY - A deed in which the grantor warrants the title against defects arising after he acquired the land but not against defects arising before that time.

DEED, TRUST - A deed which established a trust. It generally is an instrument which conveys legal title to property to a trustee and states his authority and the conditions binding upon him in dealing with the property held in trust. Frequently trust deeds are used to secure lenders against loss. In this respect they are similar to mortgages.

DEED, WARRANTY - An instrument in writing, by which title to real property is conveyed wherein the freehold is guaranteed by the grantor, his heirs, or successors.

DESCRIPTION, LEGAL - A description recognized by law which definitely locates property by reference to government surveys, coordinate systems or recorded maps; a description which is sufficient to locate the property without oral testimony.

EASEMENT - A nonpossessing interest held by one person in land of another whereby the first person is accorded partial use of such land for a specific purpose. An easement restricts but does not abridge the rights of the fee owner to the use and enjoyment of his land. Easements fall into three broad classifications, which are easement, surface; easement, subsurface; easement, overhead.

EMINENT DOMAIN - The right by which a sovereign government, or some person acting in its name and under its authority, may acquire private property for public or quasi-public use upon payment of reasonable compensation and without consent of the owner. The right or power of the government to take private property for public use on making just compensation therefor.

ENCROACHMENT - 1) A building, a part of a building, or obstruction which intrudes upon or invades a highway or a sidewalk or trespasses upon the property of another. 2) The act of trespassing upon the domain of another. Partial, or gradual displacement of an existing use by another use; as locating factories in a residential district.

ENCUMBRANCE - An interest or right in real property which diminishes the value of the fee, but does not prevent conveyance of the fee by the owner. Mortgages, taxes, and judgements are encumbrances known as liens. Restrictions, easements, and reservations are encumbrances, though not liens.

INITIAL POINT (USPLS) - The point from which the survey of the principal meridian and base line. controlling the survey of the public lands within a given area, is initiated. For a list of initial points, principal meridians. and base lines, and the areas governed thereby, see Section 139, Bureau of Land Management Manual of Surveying Instructions, 1947.

LINE, PROPERTY - The division between two parcels of land, or between a parcel of land and the street.

LINE, RANGE (USPLS)- A boundary of a township surveyed in a north-south direction.

LINE, TOWNSHIP (USPLS) - An exterior boundary of a township extending in an east-west direction.

LIS PENDENS - A notice of the pendency of an action involving real estate recorded in the registry of deeds. He who purchases during the pendency of the suit is bound by the decree that may be against the person from whom he derives the title.

MAP, CADASTRAL - A map showing the boundaries of subdivisions of land, usually with the bearings and lengths thereof and the areas of individual tracts, for purposes of describing and recording ownership. A cadastral map may also show culture, drainage, and other features relating to the value and use of land.

MERIDIAN - A north-south reference line, particularly a great circle through the geographical poles of the earth. The term usually refers to the upper branch. that half, from pole to pole, which passes through a given place: the other half being called the lower branch.

METES AND BOUNDS - A method of describing land by measure of length (metes) of the boundary lines (bounds). Most common method is to recite direction and length of each line as one would walk around the perimeter. In general the "metes" and "bounds" can be recited by reference to record, natural or artificial monuments at the corners; and record, natural or cultural boundary lines.

MONUMENT (USPLS) - A physical structure which marks the location of a corner or other survey point. In public-land surveys, the term "corner" is employed to denote a point determined by the surveying process, whereas the "monument" is the physical structure erected to mark the corner point upon the earth's surface. Monument and corner are not synonymous, though the two terms are often used in the same sense.

NORTH - The primary reference direction relative to the earth; the direction indicated by 000 in any system other than relative. True north is the direction of the north geographical pole; magnetic north, the direction north as determined by the earth's magnetic lines of force; compass north, the direction north as indicated by a magnetic compass; grid north, an arbitrary reference direction used with grid navigation.

NORTH, MAGNETIC - The direction of the north-seeking end of a magnetic compass needle not subject to transient or local disturbance.

NORTH, TRUE - A term used to define 1) an astronomic meridian; 2) a geodetic meridian; 3) the direction of north from magnetic north corrected for declination; 4) the meridional direction assumed in a survey description; 5] the cardinal directions run in the Public Land Survey. Since the term is subject to several interpretations it should not be used. See also azimuth, astronomic; azimuth, geodetic; azimuth, grid; azimuth, magnetic.

NOTORIOUS POSSESSION - Possession that is so conspicuous that it is generally known and talked of by the public or the people in the neighborhood. Possession or character of holding in its nature having such elements of notoriety that the owner may be presumed to have notice of it and of its extent.

PAROL EVIDENCE - Oral evidence; that which is given by word of mouth; the ordinary kind of evidence, given by witnesses in court. In a particular sense, and with reference to contracts, deeds, wills, and other writings, parol evidence is the same as extraneous evidence or evidence aliunde.

PATENT - An instrument conveying title to land. Usually the original conveyance of state, crown, or province land.

PRESCRIPTION - Title obtained in law by long possession. Occupancy for the period prescribed by the Code of Civil Procedure, as sufficient to bar an action for the recovery of the property, gives. title by prescription.

PUBLIC DOMAIN LANDS - The term public lands has been applied broadly to the area that was turned over to the government by the colonial states, and to the lands that were acquired later by purchase from, or treaty with the native Indians or with the foreign powers that had previously exercised the sovereignty. These large areas have been subject to administration, survey, and transfer of title under the public-land laws of the United States. The public-land laws have not been applicable within the colonial states or any of the Atlantic Coast states excepting Florida, nor within the states of West Virginia, Kentucky, Tennessee, and Texas. The public lands now include the original public-domain lands, title to which is still in federal ownership; also, lands which were obtained by the government in exchange for original public-domain lands or for timber on such lands; also, original public-domain lands which have reverted to federal ownership through operation of the public-land laws.

RETRACEMENT - A term applied to a survey that is made for the purpose of verifying the direction and length of lines, and identifying the monuments and other marks of an established prior survey.

RIGHT-OF-WAY - 1) Any strip or area of land, including surface, overhead, or underground, granted by deed or easement, for construction and maintenance according to designated use, such as for drainage and irrigation canals and ditches; electric power, telegraph, and telephone lines; gas, oil, water, and other pipe lines; highways, and other roadways, including right of portage; sewers; flowage or impoundment of surface water; and tunnels.

RIGHTS, RIPARIAN - The legal right which assures to the owner of land abutting upon a stream or other natural body of water the use of such water and the rights to the banks, bed, and travel on the water. It originated in the common law, which allowed each riparian owner to require the waters of a stream to reach his land "undiminished in quantity and unaffected in quality" except for minor domestic uses. It has been abrogated in a number of the western states, and greatly modified in others, and in general, at the present time, allows each riparian owner to make a reasonable use of the water upon his riparian land, the extent of such use being governed by the reasonable needs and requirements of other riparian owners and the quantity of water available.

SET-BACK - The term refers to zoning regulations which designate the distance a building must be set-back from the front property line; or the height at which the upper floors of a building are recessed, setback, from the face of a lower structure. In tall buildings there may be more than one set-back.

SURVEY, BOUNDARY - A survey made to establish or to re-establish a boundary line on the ground or to obtain data for constructing a map or plat showing a boundary line. The term boundary survey is usually restricted to surveys of boundary lines between political territories. For the survey of a boundary line between privately owned parcels of land, the term land survey is preferred, except that in surveys of the public lands of the United States the term cadastral survey is used.

SURVEY, CADASTRAL - A survey relating to land boundaries and subdivisions,made to create units suitable for transfer or to define the limitations of title. Derived from "cadastre," and meaning register of the real property of a political subdivision with details of area, ownership, and value. The term cadastral survey is now used to designate the surveys of the public lands of the United States, including retracement surveys for the identification and resurveys for the restoration of property lines; the term can also be applied properly to corresponding surveys outside the public lands, although such surveys are usually termed land surveys through preference.

SURVEYS, RECTANGULAR - A system of surveys, in which an area is divided by a base line intersected at right angles by a principal meridian, the intersection termed the initial point from which the partitions are subdivided into equal size townships containing 36 sections of land each.

TITLE - 1) The union of all the elements which constitute ownership, at common law divided into possession, right of possession, and right of property, the last two now, hoverer, being considered essentially the same. 2) That which constitutes a just cause of exclusive possession; the facts or events, collectively, which give rise to the ownership of property, real or personal. 3) The instrument which is evidence of a right.

TITLE, QUIET - A court action to clear title, remove clouds and establish ownership.

TITLE, QUITCLAIM - A title to property that extends no further than the title released by the grantor; a claim one may have in property without professing the title is valid.

TITLE INSURANCE - Insurance against financial loss resulting from claims arising out of defects in the title to real property, which are existent but undisclosed at the time the policy is issued by the title company. See also Torrens title system; abstract of title; certificate of title; title policy.

TITLE POLICY - A policy insuring the title to real property, issued for the protection of persons acquiring interests in real property either as owner, lender, or lessee; it insures against forgery, incompetents, insanities, and other matters that are not shown by public records; it insures the actual title of property as distinguished from the record title, such as is guaranteed in a guarantee of title. It usually does not insure location.

TITLE, SEARCH - An investigation of public records and documents to ascertain the history and present status of title to property, including ownership, liens, encumbrances, charges, and other interests.

TRAVERSE - A method of surveying in which lengths and directions of lines between points on the earth are obtained by or from field measurement, and used in determining positions of the points which it connects in series, and if tied to control stations on an adopted datum, the positions may be referred to that datum. Survey traverses are classified and identified in a variety of ways; according to methods used, as astronomical traverse; according to quality of results, as first-order traverse; according to purpose served, as geographical-exploration traverse; and according to form, as closed traverse, etc.

TRUE - In surveying, astronomy, engineering, etc., true is used to define exact, correct or actual values as differentiated from relative, measured or fictitious values, i.e., true north vs magnetic north, true sun vs fictitious sun, true altitude vs measured altitude. Depending on the use, "true" can have an exact meaning. Its use in descriptions to define direction, i.e., "thence true north," is not exact and has been subject to many interpretations. The generally accepted interpretation is that true north means a meridian determined with respect to the earths axis by astronomic methods. Since this meridian can be better defined by the terms astronomic north or geodetic north, the use of true is discouraged in this sense.

UNWRITTEN LAW - Unwritten law is the law not promulgated and recorded, but which is nevertheless, observed and administered in the courts of the country. It has no certain repository, but is collected from reports of the decisions of the courts and from the treatises of learned men.

USPLS - Terms relative to the United States Public Land Surveys.

WITNESS MARK - A material mark placed at a known distance and direction from a property corner, instrument, or other survey station, to aid in its recovery and identification.

In surveying, a witness mark is established as an aid in the recovery and identification of a survey station, or other point to which it is a witness. A mark which is established with such precision and accuracy that it may be used to restore or take the place of the original station is more properly called a reference mark in control surveys, and a witness corner in land surveys. Also called witness post or witness stake.

Appendix B

ALTA/ACSM Land Title Survey

An ALTA/ACSM Land Title survey is not required of everyone having a survey, but the guidelines provided in the pamphlet do establish basic standards that should be common to all surveys. Using the pamphlet as a reference in the Surveyor - Client relationship can help establish a positive understanding of the requirements of the survey. It will also enable the Surveyor and Client to speak the same language and, in the words of the old saying, compare apples to apples.

Minimum Standard Detail Requirements
for
ALTA/ACSM
Land Title Surveys
as adopted by
American Land Title Association
and
American Congress on Surveying & Mapping

It is recognized that members of the American Land Title Association (ALTA) have specific needs, peculiar to title insurance matters, which require particular information for acceptance by title insurance companies when said companies are asked to insure title to land without exceptions as to the many matters which might be discoverable from survey and inspection and not be evidenced by the public records. In the general interest of the public, the surveying profession, title insurers and abstracters, ALTA and the American Congress on Surveying and Mapping (ACSM) jointly promulgate and set forth such details and criteria for standards. It is understood that local variations may require local adjustments to suit local situations, and often must be applied. It is recognized that title insurance companies are entitled to rely on the survey furnished to them being of the appropriate professional quality, both as to completeness and as to accuracy. It is equally recognized that for the performance of a survey, the surveyor will be provided with appropriate data which can be relied upon in the preparation of the survey.

For a survey of real property and the plat or map of the survey to be acceptable to a title insurance company for purposes of insuring title to said real property free and clear of survey matters (except those matters disclosed by the survey and indicated on the plat or map), certain specific and pertinent information shall be presented for the distinct and clear understanding between the client (insured), the title insurance company (insurer), and the surveyor (the person professionally responsible for the survey). These requirements are:

1. The client shall request the survey or arrange for the survey to be requested and shall provide a written authorization to proceed with the survey from the person responsible for paying for the survey. The request shall specify that an Urban, Suburban, Rural or Mountain and Marsh land "ALTA/ACSM LAND TITLE SURVEY" is required, meeting the then-current accuracy standards jointly adopted by ALTA and ACSM. The request shall also designate which of the optional items listed in Table A are to be incorporated. The request shall set forth the record descrip-

tion of the property. The record description of the property, any record easements benefitting the property, the record easements or servitudes and covenants affecting the property ("Record Documents"), the names and deed data of all adjacent owners, as available, and any other documents containing desired appropriate information affecting the property being surveyed and to which the survey shall make reference shall be provided to the surveyor for notation on the plat or map of survey.

2. The plat or map of such survey shall bear the name, address, telephone number, and signature of the professional land surveyor who made the survey, his or her official seal and registration number, the date the survey was completed and the dates of all revisions, and the caption "ALTA/ACSM Land Title Survey" with the certification set forth in paragraph 8.

3. An "ALTA/ACSM LAND TITLE SURVEY" shall be an Urban, Suburban, Rural or Mountain and Marshland Survey in accordance with the then-current "Classification and Specifications for Cadastral Surveys" ("Accuracy Standards") as adopted, from time to time, by the American Congress on Surveying and Mapping and the American Land Title Association and incorporated herein by reference.

4. On the plat or map of an "ALTA/ACSM LAND TITLE SURVEY," the survey boundary shall be drawn to a convenient scale, with that scale clearly indicated. A graphic scale, shown in feet or meters or both, shall be included. A north arrow shall be shown and when practicable, the plat or map of survey shall be oriented so that north is at the top of the drawing. Symbols or abbreviations used shall be identified on the face of the plat or map by use of a legend or other means. If necessary for clarity, supplementary or exaggerated diagrams shall be presented accurately on the plat or map. The plat or map shall be a minimum size of 8 1/2 by 11 inches.

5. The survey shall be performed on the ground and the plat or map of an "ALTA/ACSM LAND TITLE SURVEY" shall contain, in addition to the required items already specified above, the following applicable information:

(a) All data necessary to indicate the mathematical dimensions and relationships of the boundary represented, with angles given directly or by bearings, and with the length and radius of each curve, together with elements necessary to mathematically define

each curve. The point of beginning of the surveyor's description shall be shown as well as the remote point of beginning if different. A bearing base shall refer to some well-fixed bearing line, so that the bearings may be easily reestablished. All bearings around the boundary shall read in a clockwise direction wherever possible. The North arrow shall be referenced to its bearing base and should that bearing base differ from record title, that difference shall be noted.

(b) When record bearings or angles or distances differ from measured bearings, angles or distances, both the record and measured bearings, angles, and distances shall be clearly indicated. If the record description fails to form a mathematically closed figure, the surveyor shall so indicate.

(c) Measured and record distances from corners of parcels surveyed to the nearest right-of-way lines of streets in urban or suburban areas, together with recovered lot corners and evidence of lot corners, shall be noted. The distances to the nearest intersecting street shall be indicated and verified. Names and widths of streets and highways abutting the property surveyed and widths of rights of way shall be given. Any use contrary to the above shall be noted. Observable evidence of access (or lack thereof) to such abutting streets or highways shall be indicated. Observable evidence of private roads shall be so indicated. Streets abutting the premises, which have been described in Record Documents, but not physically opened, shall be shown and so noted.

(d) The identifying, titles of all recorded plats, filed maps, right of way maps, or similar document which the survey represents, wholly or in part, shall be shown with their appropriate recording data, filing dates and map numbers, and the lot, block, and section numbers or letters of the surveyed premises. Names of adjoining owners as they appear of record and recorded lot or parcel numbers, recording information identifying the current description of record and similar information, where appropriate, shall be shown. The survey shall indicate platted setback or building restriction lines which have been recorded in subdivision plats or which appear in a Record Document which has been delivered to the surveyor. Parcel lines shall clearly indicate contiguity, gores, and overlaps. Where only a part of a recorded lot or parcel is included in the survey, the balance of the lot or parcel shall be indicated.

(e) All evidence of monuments shall be shown and noted to indicate which were found and which were placed. All evidence of monuments found beyond the surveyed premises on which establishment of the corners of the surveyed premises are dependent, and their application related to the survey shall be indicated.

(f) The character of any and all evidence of possession shall be stated and the location of such evidence carefully given in relation to both the measured boundary lines and those established by the record. An absence of notation on the survey shall be presumptive of no observable evidence of possession.

(g) The location of all buildings upon the plot or parcel shall be shown and their locations defined by measurements perpendicular to the boundaries. If there are no buildings erected on the property being surveyed, the plat or map shall bear the statement, "No buildings." Proper street numbers shall be shown where available.

(h) ALL easements evidenced by a Record Document which have been delivered to the surveyor shall be shown, both those burdening and those benefitting the property surveyed, indicating recording information. If such an easement cannot be located, a note to this effect shall be included. Observable evidence of easements and/or servitudes of all kinds, such as those created by roads; rights-of-way; water courses; drains; telephone, telegraph, or electric lines; water, sewer, oil or gas pipelines on or across the surveyed property and on adjoining properties if they appear to affect the surveyed property, shall be located and noted. If the surveyor has knowledge of any such easements and/or servitudes, not observable at the time the present survey is made, such lack of observable evidence shall be noted. Surface indications, if any, of underground easements and/or servitudes shall also be shown.

(i) The character and location of all walls, buildings, fences, and other visible improvements within five feet of each side of the boundary lines shall be noted. Physical evidence of all encroaching structural appurtenances and projections, such as fire escapes, bay windows, windows and doors that open out, flue pipes, stoops, eaves, cornices, areaways, steps, trim, etc., by or on adjoining property or on abutting streets, on any easement or over setback lines shall be indicated with the extent of such encroachment or projection. If the client wishes to have additional information with regard to appurtenances such as whether or not such appurtenances are independent, division, or party walls and are plumb, the client will assume the responsibility of obtaining such permissions as are necessary for the surveyor to enter upon the properties to make such determinations.

(j) Driveways and alleys on or crossing the property must be shown. Where there is evidence of use by other than the occupants of the property, the surveyor must so indicate on the plat or map. Where driveways or alleys on adjoining properties encroach, in whole or in part, on the property being surveyed, the surveyor must so indicate on the plat or map with appropriate measurements.

(k) As accurately as the evidence permits, the location of cemeteries and burial grounds

(i) disclosed in the process of researching title to the premises or

(ii) observed in the process of performing the field work for the survey, shall be shown.

1) Ponds, lakes, springs, or rivers bordering on or running through the premises being surveyed shall be shown.

6. As a minimum requirement, the surveyor shall furnish two sets of prints of the plat or map of survey to the title insurance company or the client. If the plat or map of survey consists of more than one sheet, the sheets shall be numbered, the total number of sheets indicated and match lines be shown on each sheet. The prints shall be on durable and dimensionally stable material of a quality standard acceptable to the title insurance company. At least two copies of the boundary description prepared from the survey shall be similarly furnished by the surveyor and shall be on the face of the plat or map of survey, if practicable, or otherwise attached to and incorporated in the plat or map. Reference to date of the "ALTA/ACSM LAND TITLE SURVEY," surveyor's file number (if any), political subdivision, section, township and range, along with appropriate aliquot parts thereof, and similar information shown on the plat or map of survey shall be included with the boundary description.

7. Water boundaries necessarily are subject to change due to erosion or accretion by tidal action ar the flow of rivers and streams. A realignment of water bodies

may also occur due to many reasons such as deliberate cutting and filling of bordering lands or by avulsion. Recorded surveys of natural water boundaries are not relied upon by title insurers for location of title.

When a property to be surveyed for title insurance purposes contains a natural water boundary, the surveyor shall measure the location of the boundary according to appropriate surveying methods and note on the or map the date of the measurement and the caveat that the boundary is subject to change due to natural causes and that it may or may not represent the actual location of the limit of title. When the surveyor is aware of changes in such boundaries, the extent of those changes shall be identified.

8. When the surveyor has met all of the minimum standard detail requirements for an ALTA/ACSM Land Title Survey, the following certification shall be made on the plat:

To (name of client), (name of lender, if known), (name of title insurance company, if known), (name of others as instructed by client):

This is to certify that this map or plat and the survey on which it is based were made (i) in accordance with "Minimum Standard Detail Requirements for ALTA/ACSM Land Title Surveys," jointly established and adopted by ALTA and ACSM in 1992, and includes Items _____ of Table A thereof, and (ii)

pursuant to the Accuracy Standards (as adopted by ALTA and ACSM and in effect on the date of this certification) of a(n) [insert "Urban," "Suburban," "Rural," or "Mountain/ Marshland" here]

_____Survey.

Date:_____

(signed)_____(seal)

Registration No.

Adopted by the American Land Title Association on October 17, 1992.

Adopted by the Board of Direction,

American Congress on Surveying and

Mapping on November 11, 1992.

American Land Title Association,
1828 L St., N.W., Suite 705
Washington, D.C. 20036.

American Congress on
  Surveying and Mapping
5410 Grosvenor Lane
Bethesda, MD 20814

TABLE A

OPTIONAL SURVEY RESPONSIBILITIES
AND SPECIFICATIONS

NOTE: The items of Table A must be negotiated between the surveyor and client. It may be necessary for the surveyor to qualify or expand upon the description of these items, e.g. in reference to Item 6, there may be a need for an interpretation of a restriction. The surveyor cannot make a certification on the basis of an interpretation.

If checked, the following optional items are to be included in the ALTA/ACSM LAND TITLE SURVEY:

1._____ Monuments placed (or a reference monument or witness to the corner) at all major corners of the boundary of the property, unless already marked or referenced by an existing monument or witness to the corner.

2._____ Vicinity map showing the property surveyed in reference to nearby highway(s) or major street intersection(s).

3._____ Flood zone designation (with proper annotation based on Federal Flood Insurance Rate Maps or the state or local equivalent, by scaled map location and graphic plotting only.)

4._____ Land area as specified by the client.

5._____ Contours and the datum of the elevations.

6._____ Identify, and show if possible, setback, height and bulk restrictions of record or disclosed by applicable zoning or building codes (in addition to those recorded in subdivision maps). If none, so state.

7._____ (a) Exterior dimensions of all buildings at ground level
(b) Square footage of:

_____(1) exterior footprint of all buildings, or gross floor area of all buildings, at ground level

_____ (2) other areas to be defined by the client

_____ (c) Height of all buildings above grade at a defined location.

8._____ Substantial, visible improvements (in addition to buildings) such as signs, parking areas or structures, swimming pools, etc.

9._____ Parking areas and, if striped, the striping and the type (eg. handicapped, motorcycle, regular, etc.) and number of parking spaces.

10._____ Indication of access to a public way such as curb cuts, drive ways marked.

11._____ Location of utilities serving or existing on the property as evidenced by on-site observation or as determined by records provided by client, utility companies and other appropriate sources (with reference as to the source of information) (for example):
(a) railroad tracks and sidings;
(b) manholes. catch basins, valve vaults or other surface indications of subterranean uses;
(c) wires and cables (including their function) crossing the surveyed premises, all poles on or within ten feet of the surveyed premises, and the dimensions of all crosswires or overhangs affecting the surveyed premises; and
(d) utility company installations on the surveyed premises.

12.____ Governmental Agency survey related requirements as specified by the client.

13.____ Significant observations not otherwise disclosed.

14.   _____
       _____

Appendix C

Measurements and Volumes

1 acre . . . . 43.560 square feet

1 acre . . . . 10 square chains

1 arpent . . . . 0.8507 acres (Ark and Miss)

1 arpent . . . . 0.84625 acres (Miss, Ala, Fl.)

1 arpent . . . . 0.845 acres (La)

1 arpent . . . . 30 toises

1 chain . . . . 100 links, 4 rods, 4 perches

40 chains . . . . 1/2 mile

80 chains . . . . 1 mile

1 decimeter . . . . 3.937 inches

1 dekameter . . . . 32.808 feet

1 fathom . . . . 6 feet, 1.8288 meters

1 foot . . . . 0.3048 meter

I furlong . . . . 10 chains, 660 feet, 220 yards, 1/8 statute mi., 201.168 meter

1 inch . . . . 2.54 centimeters

1 kilometer . . . . 0.621 mile

1 league (land) . . . . 3 statute miles, 4.828 kilometers

1 line . . . . 9 inch (Louisiana)

1 link (Gunter's or surveyor) . . . . . . 7.92 inches, 0.201168 meter

1 meter . . . . 39.37 inches, 1.094 yards

1 mile (statute or land) . . . . 5,280 feet, 1.609 kilometers, 80 chains

1 mile (nautical international) . . . . . . 1.852 kilometers, 1.151 statute mi., 0.999 U.S. nautical mi.

1 rod, pole, or perch . . . . 16 1/2 feet, 5.0292 meters

side of a square arpent . . . . 192.50 feet (Ark and Mo)

side of a square arpent . . . . 191.994 feet (Miss, Ala, Fl.)

1 sq rod . . . . 1/4 acre

30 toises . . . . 160 French feet

1 vara av . . . . 33.372 inches (Fl.)

1 vara av . . . . 33.333 inches (Texas)

1 yard . . . . 0.9744 meter

1065.75 feet . . . . 1000 French feet (La)

References

American Congress on Surveying and Mapping and the American Society of Civil Engineers, *Definitions of Surveying And Associated Terms,* 1978 (rev.).

American Land Title Association and American Congress on Surveying and Mapping, *Minimum Standard Detail Requirements for ALTA/ACSM LAND TITLE SURVEYS,* 1992.

Brown, Curtis M., and Robillard, Walter G., and Wilson, Donald A., *Evidence and Procedures for Boundary Location,* 2nd ed., John Whiley & Sons, New York, 1981, pg. 79.

Granfield, Mary, *Home Sweet Toxic Home,* Money magazine, Volume 21, No. 6, June, 1992, pg. 124.

McLaughlin, James B., and Robillard, Walter G., and Cooke, John C., *Boundary Law and Adjoining Landowner Disputes,* Professional Education Systems, Inc., Eau Claire, Wisconsin, 1989, pg. 16.

Index

A

acquiescence	14, 16
adjoining property	30, 56
adverse possession	3, 14, 16
agree by written consent	34
amendments	39
artificial object	30
Attorney	28

B

Banker	25
beginning	52, 58
bounds	5
buyer's options,	38

C

carpenter's level	77, 80
chain of title	44, 62
Clearinghouse for Hazardous Wastes	43
coastal wetlands	24
commencing	52
commons	2
concepts of ownership	9
concrete monument	67
corner replacement	32
corner witness markers	72
corner witness system	74
corners accessories	72
county seats	46
courthouse	46

D

deed	11, 46
deed checklist	65
Deed Room	46
Deed Books	47
dimensioning	56
disclosure laws	24
discrepancy	56, 60
disputes by agreement	34
Doomsday Book	2
drainage easements	48

E

earnest money	36
easement	47
egress	48
encroach	57
English and Roman common law	1
Environmental Assessment	43
environmental waste	41
EPA's radon hotline	43
evidence	11
evidence of ownership	16
exceptions	47, 49

F

fences, hedges, and ditches	57
feudal estates	2

G

geodetic monument	57
good working order	37

grantee   11
grantor   11

H

horizontal measurement   73

I

important references   43
ingress   48
inspections   37
intent to purchase   28, 35
iron pipes   30, 67

J

joint ownership   80

L

legal description   50, 62
legal devices   20
list of procedures   42
location map   57

M

marketable title   15
metal detector   67,81
mete   5
metes and bounds   4
metes and bounds description   51, 63
missing monuments   18
monuments   18

N

nationwide control system   8
natural objects   30

O

occupation and use   16
Offer To Purchase and Contract   36

overlaps or use by others   31, 57

P

plumb bob   76, 80
post hole digger   69
pre-survey system   7
property corner monument   67
Property Line Agreement   20,21
public domain   7

Q

Quitclaim Deed   20

R

real estate agent   23
recording agency   46
reference stakes   68
reference to map or plat   51, 62
reference to title   62
Register of Deeds   47
research   30
right-of-way   48

S

second point of beginning   53
sectionalized land surveys   7
seller's options   38
slope measurement   73
spade shovel   69
stake substitutes   79
standard form   35
Standard Provisions   36
Statute of Fraud   3
straight line   73
survey   10

Survey checklist   64

Surveyor   30

T

temporary stakes   68

the beginning   52

title defects   45

title insurance   45

title insurance examiners   10

title policies   45

title search   10, 44, 62

township   7

toxic wastes   41

triangulation   74

U

U. S. Rectangular system   7

unwritten methods of transfer   12

utility easements   48

V

value of Unwritten Title   15

void or overlap   56, 60

W

warrants   6

waste material   41

witness markers or monuments   72

written summary   53

WITNESS & CORNER MONUMENT MARKERS

Aluminum property corner marker for setting in concrete. 2" diameter with a 2" stem. Magnet is included for ease of location with metal detector. Can be used as witness marker with appropriate wording change.

Plastic witness markers. High—visibility yellow or orange with black lettering. 2" diameter with center hole. Can be used with brass tacks or spike shown. Tack is included with each marker.

Prices available on request. Can be shipped F.O.B. or billed to major credit card.

7" Galvanized aluminum spike. Use to place witness markers in ground. Can be purchased in most lumber or hardware stores.

TideRunner Publishing is committed to releasing future editions of this book that will prove to be even more useful to landowners. This is the first edition and with the next we are inviting other professionals specializing in property matters to make their contributions to these future editions. If you would like to be advised of future editions, please mail this cut—out to:

TideRunner Publishing
P.O. Box 770
New Bern, NC 28563

YOUR NAME

ADDRESS

CITY, STATE, ZIP

COMMENTS:

Mail or phone: (919) 633—6649

TideRunner Publishing
P.O. Box 770
New Bern, NC 28563

NAME

ADDRESS

CITY, STATE, ZIP

ITEM	QUANTITY	UNIT PRICE	TOTAL
Corner marker (aluminum)			
Witness marker (plastic)			
7" Spike (galvanized aluminum)			

METHOD OF PAYMENT

☐ F.O.B. ☐ Visa ☐ MC ☐ Am Ex

SUBTOTAL	
SALES TAX	
TOTAL	

Account #   Exp. Date

Signature   Phone